Letting Things Go
A Faraway Poetry Collection

Dear Reader,

I write this in dark times, in a dark
bedroom, fully aware that it's my own choice
to keep the lights off, to keep the light out.
I do not come to you a fully happy person.
I am not who I am meant to be just yet.
My hope is that, by the end of this book,
you and I end up as two different people,
better because we have felt this way.
This is a celebration, of living, losing,
and everything in between.

INTRODUCTION

Thanks for your interest in the Sam Mason Mystery Series! This series is set in small-town northern New Hampshire where anything can happen and playing by the rules doesn't necessarily mean that justice will be served. It features a small town police force and their trusty K-9 Lucy.

This is an on-going series with a completely solved mystery in each book and a lot of ongoing mysteries in the background. Don't forget to signup for my email list for advance notice on new release discounts:

https://ladobbsreaders.gr8.com

CHAPTER ONE

T he clump of moist brown earth hit the top of the casket with a thud. The hollow echo was a grim reminder of how quickly life could be snuffed out. Chief Sam Mason knew that well because inside the silvery-blue casket lay the body of one of his own. Officer Tyler Richardson.

Staring down at the casket, anger burning a hole in his chest, Sam made a silent promise to Tyler. He was going to find the person that shot him down and make him pay.

As chief of police of White Rock, New Hampshire, the responsibility for Tyler's death weighed heavily on his broad shoulders. He was supposed to serve and protect the public—and here he couldn't even keep one of his own officers from getting killed.

Tyler had only been twenty-eight—over a decade

younger than Sam—and only a few months shy of making sergeant when his life had been cut short at a routine stop. Tyler had always been one to help the next guy. Ironically, that was what had gotten him killed. He'd pulled over to help a vehicle with a flat tire. How was he to know the driver had stolen that vehicle? Or that the driver would shoot him down in cold blood and run off?

The incident had stirred up the quiet northern New Hampshire town. And this crime was cowardly. Even so, Sam had made sure Tyler got a hero's burial.

It was late spring. A time when the locals came out in droves to enjoy the good weather. A time for picnics and town celebrations. But not today. The chirping birds, budding trees, and smell of freshly dug earth and new spring grass had done nothing to ease the sorrow that clung to the crowd. Practically the whole town had come out to mourn Tyler. Dressed in shades of black and gray, they huddled in groups, the morning dew sticking in drops to their newly shined patent-leather shoes.

Across the gaping dark hole of the grave, Sam's second-in-command, Sergeant Jody Harris, stood just to the left of Tyler's family. She met his gaze, determination in her red-rimmed eyes. Whoever had killed Tyler Richardson was going to pay if Jo Harris had anything to say about it.

Tyler's mom, Irma, and sister, Clarissa, clutched

each other, staring down into the hole as if they still couldn't believe he was gone. Their tearstained faces registered a dull look of shocked disbelief. Sam could hardly blame them. The reality of Tyler's death still hadn't sunk in for him either, and he imagined it was worse for Tyler's two surviving family members.

Tyler hadn't been married and was devoted to Clarissa, who had a degenerative muscular disease. In fact, Sam was surprised she was standing, probably forcing herself to remain on her feet. The wheelchair that she'd had to rely on more and more since Sam had known her sat at the ready behind her.

Sam's chest constricted with worry about what would happen to her now. He knew Clarissa needed money for her medical condition. The family was not wealthy, and he knew Tyler spent most of his salary on Clarissa's care. Too bad they didn't have a fallen-officers fund. If they had, it would help alleviate some of the financial burden.

Sam knew Tyler's family was too proud to accept handouts, but Irma and Clarissa didn't know there wasn't a fallen-officers fund, and Sam's 401k could survive another withdrawal. Besides, he had no intention of ever retiring.

Sam caught a motion at the periphery of the crowd. Reese Hordon, the department receptionist, had her phone to her ear and was subtly waving to get his attention. The small White Rock police force had shut down the entire department so they could all attend the funeral, but crime didn't take the day off in order to pay respects to the dead, so Reese had had the calls rerouted to her cell phone just in case.

And judging by the stricken look on her face, Sam knew that had been a good idea.

Sam scanned the crowd for Kevin, their part-timer. It was just the three of them now since Reese didn't do fieldwork because she hadn't graduated yet from the academy. Kevin must have already seen Reese's signal and was heading in her direction. Sam caught Jo's eye and tilted his head toward Reese. Jo nodded.

Sam trudged over and made his final good-byes to Irma. He held her dry hand and looked into her blank eyes. "We're going to catch the guy that did this. But in the meantime I'm going to come and call on you. I have a check from the fallen-officers fund."

Something flickered in her eye. "There's a fund?" Her voice sounded hopeful.

Sam nodded. "Any officer shot in the course of duty gets a stipend. I hope it'll help you get through."

Sam made hasty good-byes to the other mourners. Like any other small-town police chief, Sam knew just about everybody in town. Couple that with the fact that he'd grown up here, and you might say he knew everyone in Coos County.

His shoulders slumped as he walked toward the black-and-white Tahoe.

Reese fell into step beside him, her black trench coat flapping as they walked. Reese had piled her thick jet-black hair on top of her head today, and it made her pale-blue eyes look huge. She'd dressed up to honor Tyler. The tips of her heels sank into the damp ground and threw her slightly off balance as they walked.

"Got a DB out at the Sacagewassett River," Reese whispered. Her tone was somber, but her step was full of energy. He knew Reese wasn't cold-hearted, but she had the same enthusiasm for the job that Sam had had when he was young. She hadn't been hardened by years of seeing people mistreat each other as Sam and Jo had.

"Any details?" Sam assumed since she'd mentioned the river that the body had been found in the water. He hated floaters. Depending how long they'd been in, it could be quite gruesome. And lots of times they were kids. Sam hoped to hell this one wasn't a kid.

Reese shook her head. "I can come along if you need an extra hand." Her eyes flicked toward the gravesite, and then she looked down, probably feeling bad about the implication that she might replace Tyler.

"Thanks, Reese. Can't. You have to graduate from the academy before I can send you out in the field."

Sam reached for the door handle of the Tahoe. It was a little beat up, but their small-town budget couldn't afford new cars, so they'd bought it used and made a deal with Al Riddell at the body shop to paint it with the police logo. It worked well enough for what they needed.

A hand fell on his shoulder as he opened the door, and he turned, looking into Jo's wide gray eyes. They were moist and flecked with concern, but a fire of anger burned deep inside them.

"Don't worry. We're going to catch the guy that did this," she said.

Sam's eyes drifted back toward the gravesite. The person that had shot Tyler had run off, and so far they had precious few leads. But Sam was making it a personal mission to bring him to justice. So was Jo.

"I know. But right now there's someone else that needs our help."

Jo nodded then hopped into the Crown Vic with Kevin. Sam started up the Tahoe and headed toward the river. The loud gunshots from the twenty-one-gun salute rang in his ears as he drove past the wrought-iron gates and out of the cemetery.

CHAPTER TWO

Jo must have broken the speed limit on her way to the river, because when Sam emerged from the woods to the side of the river, she was already ankle deep in water and squatting over the body. John Dudley from the county coroner's office was crouched beside her.

The body had washed up in the shallow part of the Sacagewassett River. The river was a lazy river that wound its way down from the Canadian border and through town. Since it was early May, the river was high with runoff from the snowy mountains. Some small sections of the river had white water that attracted rafters. Other sections ran slower, better for canoeists. The section that ran along the Rock Ledge campground flowed at a medium pace because the area was wide and shallow.

Sam figured the body had come from somewhere upstream and gotten caught up on the rocks and branches in this shallow sandbar.

He splashed across the water, which saturated his newly polished black leather oxfords and wicked up the bottoms of his navy-blue dress uniform pants. They had worn their best uniforms out of respect for Tyler today. Normally, they dressed more casually.

Sam navigated the slippery rocks, the cold water freezing his ankles. Raising his eyes from the smooth, round stones, he risked a glance north at the mountain range. In the distance, layers of blue mountains, some still with white snow peaks, jutted up into the cloud-less blue sky. He inhaled the smell of fresh running water, cleansing his mind before he had to deal with the grim scene before him. The clicking of Kevin's camera as he recorded the various aspects of the death scene added an oddly mechanical feel to the natural sounds of rushing water and twittering birds.

Jo moved aside as he approached, giving Sam a full view of the body. Sam felt a mixture of guilt and relief. It wasn't a kid, but the now-lifeless body was still someone's child. It was a young woman in her midtwenties. She wore only a pair of thin white cotton undies, and Sam thought she hadn't been in the river long, judging by the looks of things. Sam guessed about five or six hours.

"What do you think?" Sam asked.

Jo squinted up at him. John kept examining the body. Kevin kept snapping pictures. From what he could see of the body, Sam didn't know if this was an accident or something more sinister. If it was the latter, the water would have washed away key evidence. He hoped it was the former, but the burning in his gut told him otherwise.

"Hard to tell." John pointed at the side of the head where there was an obvious injury, though the water had washed away the blood that Sam knew would have otherwise been caked in the victim's hair.

"She might've died from a head wound. Could have slipped and fallen into the water, been knocked unconscious, drowned, and been carried downstream," John said.

They all looked upstream, where the water was rushing faster. Here, it had slowed down in the spot where the river widened and got curvy. Though the river wasn't very deep, you could still drown in an inch of water.

"Foul play?" Sam glanced back at the small crowd that had gathered on the bank just near the campground. People stood with their arms wrapped around themselves, a buzz of anxiety rising from the crowd as they whispered to each other while shuffling from foot to foot.

This early in the season, the campground wasn't very crowded. Things didn't really get rolling up north until after Memorial Day. The way Sam saw it, that could be good and bad. Good because there were fewer people to interview. Bad because there were fewer people that might have seen something that would tell them what happened.

"Hard to tell." John put a medieval-looking instrument back in the black bag he'd set on top of a rock and then looked up at Sam. "I have to get her back to the morgue and do an autopsy to know for sure."

Sam nodded. "Sure seems weird that she's only got her underwear on."

Jo tilted her head to look at the side of the victim's skull. "Maybe she went skinny dipping and hit her head."

"Who wears their underwear skinny dipping?" Sam eyed the gash in her skull. He doubted a fall would cause that amount of damage.

EMTs had arrived and splashed across the water toward them. John nodded to them, and they unrolled a piece of canvas that they would use to carry the body to the stretcher waiting at the riverbank. As they lifted up the body, someone screamed.

"Oh my God, it's Lynn!"

Jo stood, her eyes narrowing in on the screamer. She was studying her. That was Jo's area of expertise. Human behavior. Sam, on the other hand, was all about the evidence. He liked to take his time. Turning all the clues over in his mind to find that missing link, the oddity, the thing that gave the killer away. Jo focused on the human side. The way they acted, body language, and what they said and did. Between the two of them, they had a high success rate at catching criminals.

"Guess we know who to talk to first." Sam glanced back at John. "Are we done here?"

"Yep."

"Pictures?" Sam glanced at Kevin, who nodded, indicating he was done taking pictures.

John started across the river after the EMTs. "I'll call you with the results."

Sam, Jo, and Kevin started toward the crowd gathered on the riverbank.

"Kevin, you get names and phone numbers from everyone. Talk to Ellie and find out if anyone saw anything." Ellie was the campground manager. Sam had known her since he was a teenager. "Jo, you and I will go talk to the screamer. We'll meet you back at the station later, Kev."

Sam sucked in a breath and followed Jo toward the group of campers. He hoped to hell the girl in the river had died by accident, but his instincts told him otherwise. And if his instincts were right, one of the people in that group could be a cold-blooded killer.

CHAPTER THREE

The screamer, a blonde named Amber Huffman, was huddled with five other people all about the same age. Friends on a camping trip, Sam guessed.

"Did you know her?" Jo glanced back toward the river.

Their faces were solemn as they nodded.

"I think that's our friend Lynn Palmer," a girl with straight brown hair and a smattering of freckles said between sniffs.

Jo looked at the group with sympathy. "Are you camping here?"

"Yeah, back there." A tall guy nodded his head toward the campground.

"Maybe we should go back there and talk," Jo suggested. She herded them back toward the campground. They walked alongside her in a daze. Sam hung back, watching. They all appeared stunned by the discovery of their friend's body.

Jo took out a small pad and pencil and started writing down information, pausing every so often to swat at the swarm of black flies that had decided she'd make a good breakfast. She went through the group, asking their names and addresses, gathering little bits of information. Sam knew she was also studying them like a hawk. Looking for a twitch here or an eye jerk there that would indicate they had something to hide.

While Jo was asking the pertinent questions, Sam looked around the campsite. It was typical of what you might expect from a camping crowd of people in their early twenties. The equipment was adequate, the same kinds of things Sam would've used when he was that age. Canvas tents, Coleman lanterns, and stoves. A blue tarp stretched over each tent indicated these were experienced campers. Anyone who had camped for a few seasons knew you prepared for rain even when no clouds were in sight. Once your camping gear got wet, it never dried out.

Woodsmoke wafted over from a fire that burned in a ring of circular stones. A pan of burnt eggs sat on top of a grate to the side of the fire. Their breakfast had probably been interrupted when news of a body spread through the campground.

"And how did you hear that a body had been

found?" Jo had finished with the personal information and was starting to ask questions.

"We were finishing up breakfast." A short redhead named Tara Barrett motioned toward the picnic table where six waterproof lunch bags stood. "I had just finished packing the lunches for our hike today when we heard a big commotion, and someone yelled something about a body. We ran down and..." Her voice trailed off in a sob.

"Didn't you notice that Lynn wasn't here?" Their eyes all flew to a red tent that was situated at the base of a tall scotch pine.

"We didn't think much of it." Amber's eyes darted around to the others. "I mean, she was pretty drunk last night, and I guess we just thought she was sleeping it off."

She slipped her hand into that of a tall guy—Noah Brickey—and stepped closer to him as if for comfort.

"That's right. I was just about to check on her." The brunette, Julie Swan, blew her nose into wadded-up toilet paper she'd ripped from a roll that was sitting on the picnic table. "I never thought she'd be... well, what exactly happened to her?"

"That's what we're going to find out," Jo said. "Did any of you notice anything strange last night? Do you know why she would be in the river?"

"She probably went swimming," Tara said. "I mean, unless she hooked up with that guy from the bar."

Sam's brows shot up. "Guy from the bar?"

"We went into town last night and drank at some bar." This came from Joshua Moore, who stood next to Tara. Sam figured them for a couple. Noah and Amber were a couple, but the others looked as if they were solo. Which made him wonder, had one of them been with Lynn? Probably not on this trip if she hooked up with a guy from the bar, but maybe one of them was an ex-boyfriend.

"That place that looks like an old church," Noah added.

"Holy Spirits?" Jo asked. Holy Spirits was an old decommissioned church turned into a bar complete with original pews and altar. It was quirky and some-what of a local hangout that made the best burgers in Coos County.

"Yeah, that's the place. Anyway, Lynn met some guy there, and they seemed to hit it off. He came back here afterwards. I don't know if he was camping out or lived around here," Noah said.

"What did the guy look like?" Sam asked. He knew all the locals that hung out at Spirits.

Amber screwed up her face as if trying to conjure up an image. "Kinda long hair... and he was wearing a baseball cap. Flannel shirt, untucked."

"Was his name Jesse?" Jo asked.

Julie snapped her fingers. "Yes! That was his name."

Jo looked around at the group. "So, one of you isn't Lynn's boyfriend, then?"

"You look like couples," Sam added.

"We're not all couples." Amber clutched Noah's arm. "Me and Noah are together, and Tara and Josh are together. Everyone else is single."

"We work together at my company." Noah's voice was tinged with pride. "We make video games. We've been working our asses off to put out a new version of the game. You know, nights, weekends, hardly any time off. Our reward was to take four days off and come camping. We left a skeleton crew back at the office to keep things running." His face crumbled as if he was realizing what the reward had cost them. "Lynn worked the hardest, and she was really looking forward to kicking back and letting off some steam."

"So you saw Jesse here with Lynn?" Jo asked.

Julie made a face. "I'm not sure about that. We were partying in the bar. Then we brought the party back here. Some other people joined us for a little while. Some from that campground over there." Julie slapped at a bug on her knee then pointed through the woods to a patch of blue tent and wafting campsite smoke. "I think that guy from the bar was here, but I'm not positive."

"I am," Amber said. "I think he followed us back. I saw him with Lynn, but I'm not sure if he was still here after I went to bed."

"So, who was the last person to see her? This guy from town?" Jo asked.

They all looked around at each other.

"Hard to say. I wasn't really paying attention," Josh said.

"What do you think would make her go in the water without her clothes on?" Sam asked.

"Swimming? She did that at night. Undies only." Tara's eyes turned misty. "I always warned her not to do it alone. And she was drunk, and the river has a lot of rocks… I mean, it was an accident, wasn't it?"

Sam didn't answer. Instead, he slapped at the high-pitched whine around his ear. A mosquito. Up here, once the bloodthirsty insects got a bead on you, they came in like a squadron of fighter planes. They made a noise like an incoming missile, had the sting of a harpoon, and their bite left a lump the size of a golf ball.

Here in the dense woods, both mosquitos and black flies were out in full force, and their conversation was punctuated by waving arms as the campers swatted at them. Sam had to stop himself from scratching, or he'd have a lump five times bigger than the tiny bug that had caused it.

He glanced through the patch of woods toward the river. There was a thin path leading from the campsite toward it. "Is that where you go swimming?"

"Yeah." Noah swatted at a bug in front of his face. "But her body wasn't found there."

"She could've been carried downstream." Sam walked down the path. The beach was about fifty feet away. Very small, with a thin sandy patch hardly big enough to put a towel on. Good enough for getting your feet wet, though. He studied the area, looking for anything out of the norm. The water ran faster here. Lynn could have entered the water here. The current wasn't strong enough to sweep away anyone that could swim, but if she'd been unconscious, it would have carried her away. Maybe she'd been so drunk that she'd passed out and drowned.

"Do you see anything?" Julie ventured.

"No." Sam spun and looked at her. "But I'm wondering if Lynn went swimming on her own, then where are her clothes?"

Julie frowned and looked around. "I don't know. She was wearing a red tie-dyed shirt and cotton pants. But she could've taken them off in her tent."

"And walked half naked through the campsite?" Jo asked. "You guys must all be really good friends."

Julie frowned. "No, she wouldn't—"

"*Woof!*"

Sam turned to see a large, scraggly dog. It had the markings of a German shepherd, but it was bigger. Some kind of mix, he guessed. Maybe Rottweiler... or bear. The coat was matted, and the dog was thin, as if it hadn't eaten in a while.

A pang of sympathy for the dog shot through him. They'd seen their share of strays. Usually, they took them in and Reese posted their picture on Facebook, then Sam or Jo dropped them at the shelter. Between him and Jo, they tried to make sure extra effort was made to find the dogs' families. But this one looked as if it might not have a family.

"Is that your dog?" Sam asked.

"No. Never seen it before."

Sam turned back to the dog. Its whiskey-brown eyes looked at him as if it knew something he didn't.

The dog turned and walked a few paces into the woods back toward where they had found the body.

"I think she wants you to follow her." Jo had come to stand beside him.

Sam didn't take his eyes off the dog, who had stopped a few feet into the woods and was now looking back over its shoulder.

"Well, if you're not going to follow her, I am." Jo started after the dog.

Sam shrugged and followed. How did Jo know it was a girl? The fur was so long and matted, Sam couldn't see any of the parts that might give a clue as to the dog's gender.

The dog didn't walk far. It stopped near another beach away from any of the campsites. It pawed at something on the ground at the base of a birch tree. A pile of clothes that contained a red tie-dyed shirt.

Sam and Jo squatted to inspect the clothes. Jo pulled a latex glove out of her windbreaker and poked through the pile. Thin cotton pants, the red shirt, and a red lacy bra.

Julie had followed them. They turned to her. "Is this the shirt?"

Julie nodded, her eyes filling up. "Those are hers. Those are Lynn's clothes."

"She must have taken them off here and gone for a swim from the beach there." Jo nodded toward a thin stretch of sand at the edge of the river. Here the river was wider and deeper. Probably about four feet in the middle.

Sam stood and turned around, assessing the area. It was away from other campsites. Private. "If she were meeting someone and wanted some privacy to go skinny-dipping, this would be the place."

Jo squinted up at him. "If she was meeting some-one, we need to find out who. He could have been the last person to see her alive."

Sam's eyes met Jo's. "Or the first person to see her dead."

CHAPTER FOUR

Sam drove back to the police station after interviewing the people at the surrounding campsites. They'd given a similar story. No one had been paying attention to Lynn. They'd all been busy drinking and partying it up. They'd all gone to bed around two a.m., or so they said. Since Sam had no idea when Lynn had died, he couldn't very well be pressing them for alibis.

Not that he needed alibis at this point. The death could simply be an accident that wouldn't require an investigation.

According to the campers, Lynn Palmer had been from Massachusetts. Too far for him to do the notification to her family. It broke his heart to think that somewhere down there the local cops would be informing Lynn's parents of her death. He hated leaving that job to someone else, but the best thing he could do for them now was figure out what had happened in the last hours of their daughter's life.

Downtown White Rock was your typical northern New Hampshire town. Brick and concrete buildings accented with fine architectural details lined the main street. Most of the buildings dated to the early 1900s, but the town had been kept up, so they weren't in disrepair.

In the middle of Main Street, a grass median ran the length of the block where most of the town offices stood. In the center of the median sat a statue of the town's first mayor, Hiram White, mounted on a horse. Little kids liked to climb on the horse. The statue was often pranked by older kids who would outfit the long-dead mayor with quirky hats and, sometimes, stick mannequins or straw dummies on the back of the horse.

It was mostly all in fun, except for the time someone put a naked blow-up doll on the back and almost caused a fit of the vapors amongst the town biddies. The police station phone had rung off the hook that morning.

Like most small towns, the government offices had to make do with what they had. The police station had recently moved from the basement of the town hall to the old post office. The post office had gotten its own fancy new building. Apparently, mail was a priority over crime fighting in White Rock.

Sam liked the post office building. The building dated to the 1930s and had somehow managed to retain the black-and-white swirly marble floors and original oak moldings with carved details. It still smelled of old paper and stamp glue, which was a welcome improvement over the musty basement of the town hall.

As an added bonus, the post office had left most of their furniture behind. Even the old bronze post office boxes still sat in their oak wall, creating a partial divider between the reception area and what had become the squad room. Each box had twin dials at the top with gold numbers on a black background. Below the dials, a fancy embossed eagle with a US shield on its chest sat proudly amidst fluted rays that extended to the edge of the box. Below the eagle, a small beveled glass window let you see how much mail was inside.

Sam couldn't understand why the post office had opted for ugly new plain metal boxes instead of taking the old ones, but he didn't question it. Some people had no taste. The bank of one hundred twenty boxes made a perfect divider, and Reese used them to organize the various pieces of mail, tax payments she collected, and copies of the permit applications she issued.

Beyond the wall of post office boxes was the squad

room. It used to be the mail sorting area and was one open room with three oak craftsman-style desks. The desks were scarred from decades of use, but the honey-colored stained wood still glowed. They were solid wood, not like the plywood junk they had today.

He rounded the bank of post office boxes and stopped short. Jo was on the floor, hand-feeding pot roast from the diner across the street to the dog.

"You know we're supposed to turn him in to the shelter," Sam said.

"Her."

Sam looked at the dog and raised a brow. Jo sounded sure of the dog's sex, so he went with it.

She continued, "And technically we're supposed to turn them in at the *first available opportunity*."

More brow raising from Sam.

Jo shrugged. She was used to his unspoken messages. After four years of working closely together, they could practically read each other's minds. "I haven't had an *opportunity* yet. I've been following up on some of the things we learned this morning."

As if to corroborate this, the dog looked up at Sam with innocent eyes.

"Seeing as we're shorthanded now, I may not have time to bring her for a while." Jo's words had them both glancing at Tyler's empty desk. Sam's stomach tightened. Not only had he lost a good friend and a damn good officer, but now they were shorthanded, meaning they would have to work extra.

He thought about Lynn Palmer. If she'd been murdered, he wanted to be able to do right by her, and that would be harder with one less officer. On the other hand, he couldn't even think about someone else filling Tyler's shoes right now. It was too soon.

"Where's Kevin?" he asked.

"He left for the day. You know how he is. Doesn't like to put in a lot of hours." Jo pushed up from the floor and dusted off her pants. She had taken off her police belt, and it lay on her desk with all the bulky accoutrements. "Are you going to bring him on full time?"

Sam pressed his lips together. The dog finished lapping up the pot roast and came over and pressed herself against his leg. He rubbed her silky ears absently. Though the dog's fur was dirty and matted, the ears felt like fine satin sheets on Sam's fingertips. "I suppose so. Seems like the right thing to do since he's been here with us for a while now."

"Yeah. Don't know if he'll want it, though." Jo went over to her desk and plopped into the old Naugahyde-and-steel chair that had been left there when the post office vacated. Sam had a chair just like it. He thought they dated to the 1950s, but they were comfortable and still did the job. Why get new ones when these worked just fine?

Jo was right about Kevin—he wasn't exactly ambitious, though he did do an adequate job. Truth be told, Sam wouldn't be disappointed if Kevin didn't want the full-time job, but he'd offer it to him just the same when he was ready because it was the right thing to do.

"So what do you make of it?" Sam didn't need to elaborate. Jo would know that he was referencing the campers and the body from the river.

"Could just be an accident. She could've gone swimming and passed out or slipped and hit her head. But I'm having Reese do some digging into the friends she was camping with just in case."

As per protocol with a death that was not natural, they'd blocked off the areas where Lynn's body and clothing had been found with crime scene tape. They weren't sure if it was a crime scene yet, but better safe than sorry.

Since Kevin had left before they'd discovered the pile of clothes, Sam had shot pictures of the area with his cell phone. Kevin would have to go back and take better pictures later. He used a Nikon digital camera, and the pictures came out a lot better than Sam's blurry ones that were usually marred by a close-up of his thumb obscuring the subject of the picture.

"I got that information you wanted." Reese peeked around the corner of the post-office-box wall, and the dog trotted over to her, her burr-infested tail swishing back and forth enthusiastically.

"Good girl, Lucy." Reese bent down, scratching the dog behind her ears. The fur on the edges of her ears was matted, and the insides of her ears red.

"You named her?" Sam asked.

"We can't just call her 'it,'" Reese pointed out.

"She's not going to be here that long. We have to take her to the shelter." Sam didn't like the way the dog narrowed her eyes at him, the whiskey-brown color turning to a sad shade of brown in the slanting light coming in from the windows.

Lucy switched her attention from Reese to Sam. She trotted over and pressed herself against his leg, looking up at him with those pleading eyes. Sam tried to resist the look. He was good at resisting it in women, and he figured resisting it in dogs should be even easier. It wasn't.

"I posted her on Facebook already." Reese had sat in an empty chair, her laptop in her lap. Her bloodred fingernails clacked on the keyboard. "Hopefully, someone will claim her soon and she won't have to go to the shelter. Jo said she helped you guys find a clue—she deserves special treatment. Anyway, check out the information I found."

"Information?" Sam tried to ignore the way Lucy was putting her head under his hand, trying to force him to pet her.

"Jo asked me to look into this gaming company that

the campers work at. Lyah Games." She turned the computer screen toward him.

"And?" Sam asked. Reese was a fairly new addition to his staff, but Sam had already noticed she had above-average computer skills. Even though he couldn't let her do field work, there was no rule about letting her use the Internet.

"The company is legit. And the people Jo had in her notes are listed on their informational page. Well, most of them are." She angled the screen toward Sam, and he recognized five of the campers' names on the list of the company's officers:

NOAH BRICKEY - CEO
 Lynn Palmer - COO
 Tara Barrett - CFO
 Joshua Moore - Director, Software Engineering
 Julie Swan - Director, Human Resources

"THAT'S MOST OF THEM. Guess the others didn't rate," Sam said.

"They do make video games just like they said, but check this out." Reese swiveled the laptop back to face her, tapped on the keyboard some more, then swung it back to Sam. The screen showed a bunch of figures that were like Greek to him.

"They're not doing very well financially," she explained.

Sam squinted at the screen. "Is that what that means?" He frowned up at Reese. "Did you get this information legally?"

Reese rolled her eyes. "Of course. It's a company prospectus. Public knowledge."

"That's interesting," Jo said. "But why would that motivate one of them to kill her? Lots of companies are doing poorly, and he did say they just worked really hard to get a new release out."

"Good question. But at least now we know they weren't lying about their work," Sam said. "Whether or not they were lying about anything else remains to be seen."

CHAPTER FIVE

S am's office was large. It had three ten-foot-tall windows with round tops that looked out over the town toward the White Mountains. The floor was wide pine boards scuffed by decades of use. The walls were thin strips of oak wainscoting on the bottom and a municipal green paint on the top. The old oak-paneled door with smoked glass window was original to the post office. Only the gold-and-black lettering had been changed from Postmaster to Chief of Police.

His desk was a long double-wide partners desk made of oak. By the amount of staples embedded in it and the blue-ink postmark stamps that tattooed the surface, it seemed the post office must have used it to sort and stamp mail. Sam used it to spread out his case files on.

It was late in the afternoon. Sam was leaned back in

his office chair with his hands clasped behind his head and his feet propped up on the desk, thinking about the girl in the river, when John called with the bad news.

"I got the time of death. Between 2:15 and 2:45 a.m. Your victim didn't drown, though. No water in the lungs."

Sam swung his feet onto the floor, sitting upright in the chair. "It's sounding like you don't think she died by accident."

"Cause of death was a massive blow to the head. I don't think she could've done that to herself. She could have fallen and slipped on the rocks, but she wouldn't have hit with the kind of force needed to kill her right away. Knock her out, sure. But with no water in the lungs, she didn't drown. That blow killed her." John paused to take a breath. "Not only that, but judging by the abrasions and contusions on her body, she was killed in one place and dragged to another. This was done post mortem. My guess is the killer was hoping she'd wash downriver, maybe even out of town, but she ended up getting stuck on the shallow sandbar instead."

As Sam digested this information, he glanced out the window to see the mayor, Harley Dupont, walking toward the building. A bad day was turning worse. There was no love lost between Dupont and Sam. Dupont had been a few years behind Sam all through high school. He hadn't liked him back then, and he'd liked him even less when Dupont had returned to White Rock to practice law a few years after getting his fancy Harvard education.

He'd been a pain in Sam's ass ever since he became mayor four years ago. Judging by the determined look on his face, Sam knew he was fixing to be a pain in his ass right now, too.

Sam hung up with John and went out into the main area to give Jo and Reese the bad news. "Looks like Lynn Palmer was murdered."

Jo didn't look up from the pile of papers on her desk. A coffee mug sat half empty next to her, a jelly donut with one bite left beside that. "Not surprised. Already on it."

Reese wasn't as seasoned or jaded—her eyes softened. Her face showed compassion, and her hands reached instinctively for the dog, which was seated beside her desk. Before she could say anything, the door opened and Dupont walked in.

His suit was impeccable, his reddish hair parted on the side and combed over the slightly balding spot in front. His beady brown eyes flicked from Reese to Sam to Jo, looking at them as if they were the broccoli side dish on his plate that his mother was about to force him to eat.

Lucy got to her feet and growled.

Dupont's eyes jerked toward the dog, whose body was rigid, her attention focused on Dupont as if he were a threat. Sam's estimation of the dog went up tenfold. She was a good judge of character.

Dupont planted his fake mayoral smile on his face but kept his eyes trained on Lucy. "What's a dog doing here? You're not allowed to have pets in here."

Reese put a restraining hand on Lucy's neck. The dog stayed where she was. "She's not a pet. She's a stray. We're looking for her owners." The tone in Reese's voice told Sam that she liked Dupont about as much as Sam did. Good girl.

"Strays are supposed to be at the pound." Dupont's eyes softened just a tad as he looked at the dog again. Or was Sam imagining that?

"And that's where we're going to take her as soon as we get freed up," Sam said. "In case you didn't know, we have a murder to investigate."

Dupont straightened his jacket and looked away from Lucy. "I know. In fact, that's why I'm here. Nadine and Thomas Palmer are good friends of mine, and I want to assure them that everything will be done to bring their daughter's killer to justice."

Sam resisted the urge to roll his eyes. "We always do our best."

"I want this investigation done by the book." Dupont held a hand up at Sam's narrow-eyed look. "Let's not pretend here. I know how you like to take things into your own hands, sometimes, but I want your full attention on this case, and I want it done right." He leaned toward Sam, his voice lower. "The Palmers are very influential, and my reputation as mayor is on the line... and I wouldn't want to have to resort to tarnishing *your* reputation as chief of police to keep mine polished. I'm sure you wouldn't want your daughters to have to hear about your previous screw-ups."

Dupont didn't have to elaborate. The reference to what had happened twenty years ago when he was still in the police academy made Sam's blood boil. The vaguely threatening mention of Sam's twin daughters pissed him off even more. Sam's hands tightened into fists, but he shoved them into his pockets instead of punching Dupont in the face as he wanted to. He struggled to make his voice even toned and pleasant. "Of course. We want justice just as much as anyone else."

Dupont studied Sam for a minute, the two men staring at each other like two gunslingers in the town square at high noon.

Dupont blinked first. "I expect frequent updates." He spun and strode to the door then turned back and looked at Lucy. "And get rid of the dog."

CHAPTER SIX

J o tapped the end of her pencil forcefully on the desk, taking her frustrations out on the pink rubber eraser. She spun in her chair to watch Dupont walk away from the building. The guy was a jerk. Not only did he act like a pompous ass, but he had no respect for anyone on the police force.

This wasn't the first time Dupont had thrown a veiled threat at Sam. Jo had no idea what Dupont was talking about, but she could tell by Sam's reaction that the threat had hit home. Something had happened in Sam's past, but she had no idea what it was.

Jo had been able to tell that Sam was holding back from popping Dupont in the face. Couldn't blame him. Heck, she wanted to punch him herself. She'd seen the tells in Sam's body language. The way his shoulders stiffened. How he'd clenched his large hands into fists, and from where she was seated, she could just see the tick in his strong jaw even through the thick stubble that covered it. Sam hid his emotions well, but he couldn't hide them from her—she was an expert at reading people.

Jo had no intention of delving into what, exactly, Dupont had been referring to, though. She had her own skeletons that were better left in the closet with the door firmly shut. She wouldn't want anyone prying into her past business, so she wouldn't pry into Sam's. If he wanted her to know, he'd tell her.

Sam was a good cop and a good person. The kind of person that you wanted to have on your side. The kind of person that would have your back no matter what. That was all she needed to know, and if Sam had done something in the past that was the cause of Dupont's threats, she was sure it had been for a good reason.

Dupont, on the other hand, was not a good person. Taking a jab at Sam's kids was a low blow. She knew Sam loved his twin daughters more than anything. They were in college now. Nice girls. Still young and innocent. To make a threat like that just proved what an asshole the mayor was.

"Don't listen to anything Dupont said. He's an ass clown," she said.

Sam sighed and dropped his hand to Lucy's head. "Even a dog knows that."

Jo looked at the German shepherd mix wistfully. No

one had responded to the Facebook post claiming her, and she knew they would have to take her to the shelter before the end of the day.

As if reading her mind, Reese said, "She's smart. It'd be a shame to take her to the shelter. Maybe one of you guys needs a pet?"

"I wish," Jo said. "I'm renting my place, and pets aren't allowed."

Jo was a loner by nature, but another living creature might be nice to have at home. Something soft and furry, preferably. But the landlord had been very clear about that. She liked her little cabin up in the woods and didn't want to get evicted. Maybe a goldfish would have to do.

Reese's gaze flicked to Sam. He owned his own home, an old hunting camp he'd inherited from his grandfather.

Sam looked at Lucy. "Sorry, girl, I don't have time for a dog."

He spread his arms to indicate the squad room. "I spend most of my time either here or out on calls. It just wouldn't be fair to her."

"I suppose you're right." Reese glanced at the computer and hit the return key. "No one has posted to claim her or that they know who she belongs to."

"There's still time. People are just getting home from work. I can drop her by the shelter if you want," Sam said.

"No. I'll do it. Eric's working there tonight, and he'll make sure that she gets another good meal and one of the good kennels." Eric was Reese's boyfriend. He was going to veterinarian school and volunteered at the animal shelter. Jo felt a little better knowing Lucy would have someone to make sure she got good treatment. Hopefully, her family would show up and claim her, though with the way her coat looked and how hungry she'd been, Jo had misgivings about turning the dog over to her family. If she had one, they weren't treating her very well.

Jo leaned back in her chair and crossed her arms. "Now that we have a murder to investigate, what do you suggest we do next, Chief? I'm sure Dupont will be scrutinizing our every move."

She already knew what *she* thought they should do next, but she wanted to see if Sam was in sync with her.

Four years of working together had put them on the same wavelength. They were usually on the same page as to what to do, and they did their jobs efficiently. Now, with Tyler gone, they'd have to be even more efficient. Her stomach clenched at the thought of the dead officer. Just because they had this murder to investigate didn't mean she was going to forget about Tyler's case. His killer was still at large.

"At least Dupont won't get in our way and impede the investigation like he usually does," Sam said.

Jo nodded. It was weird how Dupont would often muck up the works for them. Especially if they were investigating something that had to do with the builder in town, Lucas Thorne.

Thorne had come to town a few years ago. The head honcho of a real estate development company, he was hell bent on buying up all the pristine land in town so he could tear down the trees and build a large resort. Hotels, restaurants, golf courses. Nothing was safe from him, and when people didn't want to sell their old farms that had been in the family for generations, he somehow changed their minds.

Jo and Sam had a sneaking suspicion that he was also responsible for the influx of drugs coming into the community, but they hadn't been able to prove anything.

Any time they had any sort of an investigation going, it had been thwarted by Dupont, who had the ear of Judge Thompson, who would become suddenly reluctant to sign the necessary search warrants. But even though they had never been able to prove anything against Thorne, that didn't stop them from trying.

Sam turned around. "Forget about him. We have an investigation, and it's almost quitting time."

"Which makes it the perfect time to question one of our leads." Jo glanced out the window at the small stone-and-wood church wedged in between two tall brick buildings. It was one of the oldest, if not *the* oldest, buildings in town. Old-timers said the people who settled the town were religious and had built the church first so they'd have a place to worship, then the rest of the town had sprung up around it.

Religion must have gone out of style, though, because the old church had been decommissioned, and it was now a bar frequented by the locals. One of those locals was Jesse Cowly, who the campers had described as having been with Lynn the night before.

"What do you say we go grab a beer?" Sam asked.

"What a great idea." Jo tossed her pencil down on the desk and stood.

CHAPTER SEVEN

Sam had discovered long ago that he got more information out of people in the bar when he didn't show up in his police uniform. Even though everyone in town knew he was the chief of police, apparently when he was in his civvies they saw him as just plain old Sam. He preferred wearing jeans and a tee shirt anyway. So did Jo.

It didn't take Jo long to change. She came out of the bathroom in a gray long-sleeved jersey and jeans. The outfit wasn't fancy, but the color of the shirt highlighted her gray eyes and her coppery-brown hair. He didn't know what she'd done to her hair. She usually wore it stuffed up under a baseball cap, but she'd ditched the cap and fluffed it up in the bathroom, and now the mass of curls framed her head like a halo. A few silver strands had snuck in at the temples since she'd first come to work for him, but somehow they looked good on her.

Jo didn't go in for a lot of primping. She was attractive without having to put any effort into it. She wasn't a glamorous stunner like Sam's second wife, Evie, but Jo had a down-to-earth charm that shone through without having to build it up with lots of makeup and fancy hairstyles.

Jo grabbed her black leather biker jacket off the peg. She shrugged into it, the buckle-and-zipper-clad jacket falling just below her slim hips. It was still chilly at night, but Sam suspected she wore it more to hide the gun that was nestled in her belt at her waist than to ward off the cold.

Sam wore his own leather jacket. A dark-brown bomber jacket with a shearling collar that he'd picked up at the army-navy store. He'd worn the same style almost all his adult life. Evie had tried to get him to wear something more sophisticated. A shiny thin leather coat that reminded Sam of a leisure suit. Thing was, Sam wasn't sophisticated. The jacket didn't take, and he quickly went back to wearing his old comfortable bomber jacket. That was just one of the reasons why Evie was his *ex*-wife.

They spilled out onto the street. The late-afternoon rays of the setting sun gave the town a yellow glow and made Jo's curls shine like a new penny. Sam noticed a few new laugh lines were forming at the corners of her eyes.

She caught him looking and made a face. "What?"

"Nothing."

She smirked and punched him playfully in the arm as they fell in step beside each other.

They had an easy relationship. Closer than most who worked together. Even though there wasn't a lot of crime in their town, there had been a few tense situations, and Sam and Jo had learned to trust each other with their lives. That tended to create a special bond. There was nothing sexual about it. Sam didn't want to go there. He valued having Jo in his life, and after two failed marriages, Sam was done with commitments.

Holy Spirits—or just Spirits, as the locals called it— still looked like a church on the outside and was often mistaken as such. Out-of-towners who opened the tall front doors seeking a quiet place to pray got a big surprise at what they found inside.

The church wasn't big, but the twenty-foot-high ceilings gave it a spacious feel. The atmosphere was dim. Lights low. The dark wooden floors were scarred, scraped, and stained. The walls were large fieldstone about halfway up, the mortar marred with cracks and patches where it had been repaired. The noise was a constant hubbub with the drone of a low-playing jukebox in the background. Sometimes it got rowdy, but tonight it was fairly quiet.

Four of the original pews had been rearranged so as to act as seating for long tables in the back. Up front, there were several round tables with maple captain's chairs around them. Half of those tables were occupied with locals, full mugs of foam-topped beer in front of them.

Sam and Jo headed toward the bar at the back where the altar used to be. It ran the length of the small building. The windows high up on the wall behind it had been fitted with red, blue, and green stained glass in a pattern of squares and rectangles—the original church windows had disappeared long ago. The new stained glass didn't let much light in, which was exactly the way the owner, Billie Hanson, wanted it. She said dim lighting encouraged more drink purchases.

Under the stained-glass windows, colorful bottles of booze were lined up in front of a mirror that reflected the room behind them.

The seats around the bar were worn but comfortable. Sturdy wood with black pleather seat cushions edged with giant brass tacks. The bar itself was pitted and scarred with burn holes from when they used to allow smoking inside. The smell of grilled meat and french fries made Sam's stomach grumble.

Billie came to stand in front of them on the other side of the bar, her short-cropped gray hair sticking up in a blue-and-lavender-tinged spike on top. She wore one diamond stud in her left ear and a gold hoop in her right.

Her face, weatherworn from years of hard outdoor work, crinkled into a smile. Like most of the town residents, Billie had spent her lifetime outdoors doing manual labor. Her parents had owned a dairy farm, which she'd worked at year round. Now, in her sixties, she'd sold off the farm after her folks had died and bought the bar from the previous owner.

Billie could usually be found behind the bar during business hours. Most everyone called her Reverend Billie, but she wasn't a real reverend. Not unless you counted the certificate she'd gotten from the online Church of Good Will that hung behind the bar. She thought the title went great with the ambiance of the bar. She'd worked hard to build up the business, focusing on pouring a good drink and making the best gourmet burgers in the area.

Her left brow quirked up. She wiped chapped hands on her apron. "The usual?"

Sam and Jo both nodded. As Billie walked away, Jo leaned over the bar and yelled, "Add some curly fries to that, will ya?"

Billie raised a hand in acknowledgement and kept walking toward the beer fridge.

"Some day, huh?" Jo asked.

Sam huffed out of breath and nodded. It was hard to

believe that the day had included Tyler's funeral, a death scene, and a run-in with the mayor.

Billie slid two beers in front of them. A Moosenose in a green bottle for Sam. Sam liked supporting local businesses, and this one was a local brew with a slightly lemony flavor that Sam had acquired a taste for. Jo got a Sam Adams Boston Ale.

"Have you heard any more about Tyler's case?" Jo slipped a fingernail under the corner of her beer label and started picking at it.

"Not yet." They weren't supposed to be investigating Tyler's case on their own—the state police had already done an investigation, which had turned up nothing. But sometimes you needed to take matters into your own hands to make sure justice was served. Problem was, they didn't have much to go on. The car that Tyler had pulled over to help had been stolen, the owner a little old lady that lived a few towns over.

Sam figured the killer hadn't wanted to be arrested for driving a stolen vehicle and had shot Tyler then disappeared.

"I still think we can find someone who saw something. That killer must've gotten a ride from someone. That stretch of road is too far away from anything for him to have gone anywhere on foot," Jo said.

This far north, most of the roads were remote. Houses were spaced far apart. Tyler had been up at the north end of town, almost to the Canadian border.

There would've been no one around for miles to see what happened.

"Whoever it was must've been smart enough to wipe the car clean," Sam said.

The car had been wiped of fingerprints. The only thing they'd found was a partial print in the ashtray along with a dusting of cocaine. Sam figured they'd had drugs in the car. The cocaine might've come out of a bag they were stashing in the ashtray. They must have been in a hurry to get out of there after the shooting. Maybe the bag ripped in the killer's haste to grab it out of the car, and some cocaine spilled out. "Seems like if someone knew enough to wipe for prints, they would've been a criminal with a record, but we didn't get a match from the database for the partial."

"Poor Tyler probably didn't know what he was stumbling onto," Jo said.

Hadn't he? Sam wondered about that. There were a few discrepancies, like the fact that he hadn't pulled his gun and that he'd been shot right in front of the police cruiser. If the killer had come out of the stolen car with a gun, wouldn't Tyler have pulled his? It was hard to know exactly—Tyler hadn't logged the stop in his logbook, so there were no notes as to why he was pulling over. Sam just assumed his intention had been to help the disabled vehicle.

"We'll get to the bottom of it." Sam glanced sideways at Jo. Logging a stop was police protocol. Usually,

L A DOBBS

they called in or logged it in a book. That time of night, there was no one in the squad room to take the call, so they each carried a logbook. Sometimes they bent the rules a little and logged things after the stop—when they got back to the station. Except for Tyler—there was no "after." He never made it back to the station. Jo had forged the log in his notebook to avoid a black mark on his reputation during the state investigation. "By the way, thanks for covering for Tyler."

Jo shrugged. "We look out for each other, right?" She spun her chair around so that she was facing out into the main bar. She looked relaxed, casual. But Sam knew she was recording every detail of what was going on in the bar inside that superior brain of hers.

Her eyes widened, and she jerked her head toward the door as Billie slid a basket of fries across the bar to her. Sam turned to see Mick Gervasi, private investigator and his best friend since grade school, saunter in.

Mick was wearing a black jacket, leather like Jo's but bulkier. His dark hair was cut in a short military style. His clear-blue eyes scanned the bar much like Jo's but for a totally different reason. Mick didn't trust anyone, and he was looking around to see if there might be trouble he wanted to avoid.

A slight smile ticked up the corners of his lips as he spotted them. He headed toward the bar and slipped into the seat beside Jo.

Billie slid a tumbler half full of amber liquid and ice

in front of him before his jean-clad ass even settled into the seat. Whiskey. Jack Daniels, to be exact. Mick was a regular.

Jo spun back around, and the three of them hunched forward, their elbows on the bar, leaning in toward each other with Jo in the middle. Sam had hired Mick to do a little investigating into Tyler's shooting, and Jo was totally on board.

The investigation by the state police wasn't going anywhere, and Sam and Jo technically weren't supposed to be getting involved. Conflict of interest or some damn thing. They weren't about to let strangers handle Tyler's investigation, but they had to be careful how involved they got. That was where Mick came in.

"So what have you got?" Jo picked up a fry and slid her eyes toward Mick.

Mick took a swig from the tumbler. The condensation had already dripped down from the sides of the glass to form a wet ring on the bar. He put the glass back down exactly on top of the ring.

"Not much. I'm digging into all the relatives and connections for Barbara Bartles. I'm thinking maybe her car wasn't stolen by a stranger." Mick shrugged and looked out over the bar. "But I haven't come up with anything concrete yet."

Sam swigged his beer. It was cold, slightly bitter with the lemony tang. He thought about the car that Tyler had pulled over. It was a late-model Ford. The registration in the glove compartment said it belonged to Barbara Bartles, who turned out to be an elderly woman. She claimed the car had been stolen the day before.

They sat in silence for a few minutes. Jo munched on fries and scanned the room by looking in the mirror behind the bar. "Here he comes."

She swung around in her chair again, her elbows on the bar as a young guy with thin brown hair pulled back into a ponytail slid in between her and Mick to capture Billie's attention.

Jesse Cowly leaned across the bar, his long ponytail swinging to the side and brushing her arm. He glanced at her out of the corner of his eye. Sam could see he was already trying to turn on the charm, his smile wide as he looked at Jo's cleavage. Then his eyes trailed up to her face and widened with surprise when he recognized who she was.

"Hey, Jesse, you're just the person we've been looking for." Jo's words caused a flicker of concern in Jesse's eyes.

If he was guilty of something, he was good at hiding it, though. He squared his shoulders and gave Sam and Jo a blank look. "Oh? Why is that?"

"Heard you were partying with some campers last night," Jo said.

"Yeah, so? Is there a law against that now?" He grabbed a longneck from Billie and slapped a few bills on the bar then took a step back, still facing Jo and Sam.

"No law against partying," Sam said. "But when one of the other partiers gets murdered…"

Jesse's brows shot up. "Murdered? Hey, wait a minute. I didn't have anything to do with any murder."

Sam glanced at Jo. Jesse seemed panicked enough to be telling the truth, but that was more Jo's area. He knew she'd be studying his body language.

"But you were with them, right? One of them was named Lynn. Do you remember her?" Jo asked.

Jesse scratched the back of his neck. "I remember them. They were here in the bar. You can ask anyone. So what? Lots of people were in the bar."

"Yeah, but you went back to the campsite with her, didn't you?" He was acting cocky now. Arrogant. It reminded Sam of his cousin's trial almost twenty years ago. Those guys had been cocky and arrogant, too. Until Sam and Mick had stepped in with their own brand of justice.

Jesse frowned. "What is this? Are you interrogating me? You can't just come in here and ask me questions without reading me my rights or something."

Sam put up his hands palms out and plastered an easy smile across his face. "We're not interrogating you. We're sitting here in the bar having a conversation. If we wanted to interrogate you, we'd bring you into the police station. We just want to know what you saw out there at that campsite."

"I didn't see anything because I wasn't at the campsite. I was here in the bar all night. I never went out there, so whoever you got your information from is lying."

Jesse stormed off, and Jo and Sam exchanged a look.

"Well, looks like *someone* is lying," Sam said.

Jo turned back toward her beer. "They usually do when it comes to murder. The hard part is figuring out who's doing the lying and why."

CHAPTER EIGHT

O n the way home from Spirits, Sam couldn't help thinking about the dog, Lucy. The shelter was on his way, and it was still open, so he swung by just to make sure Lucy was doing okay. Hopefully, she'd be gone, picked up by her family.

She hadn't been picked up, but Eric had taken good care of her, and she was nestled in a thick sherpa-fleece-lined dog bed in the corner of a squeaky-clean kennel. Someone had washed her and groomed out the mats, and her fur shone like silk.

Sam squatted in front of the kennel door, and Lucy trotted over, eagerly sniffing his hand.

"Hey, girl, you're looking good." She smiled and looked up with hopeful whiskey eyes.

Sam patted her between the bars then stood and turned away.

Lucy whined.

Sam turned back. She was seated on her haunches, her tail swishing back and forth and those eyes looking right into his soul.

"Sorry, I can't take you home. You wouldn't like it. You'd be alone every day and most nights, too."

Lucy shot him a recriminating look. When it became clear that he wasn't there to spring her from the kennel, she turned her back on him and curled up in the bed, facing the other way.

Sam headed to his hunting cabin. He'd inherited it from his grandfather, and it was his own slice of heaven on earth. It wasn't big, just two bedrooms and a loft, but it had plenty of room for him and his daughters when they came to stay.

Evie had hated the place. She'd said it was too far out in the woods. She hated the deer-head mount that hung on the fieldstone fireplace and said it always seemed to be watching her with its black eyes. The taxidermy fish that dotted the rounded log walls freaked her out.

Funny thing, those were all the things Sam loved about the place. Especially the fish. Gramps had been an avid angler, and Sam still remembered the day Gramps had let him help pull the giant salmon they nicknamed Charlie out of Lake Howard. Charlie had gone on to win the county ice-fishing prize—five thousand dollars—that season, and he now hung proudly displayed on the wall above the overstuffed couch.

Evie had refused to live here. They'd bought a big old house closer to town, and she'd pestered him to sell the cabin, but he'd hung on. Good thing, too, because the cabin had outlasted her. Maybe Sam had always known that would be the case.

Sam tossed his keys on the aluminum fish-shaped tray beside the door and headed for the fridge, where another beer awaited. A feeling of calm settled over him as it always did when he was at the cabin. It was still pretty much the way Gramps had left it. The way he remembered it being his whole life. Since Evie had taken all their combined furniture in the divorce, he'd simply moved right into the cabin and left it as it had been when he inherited it.

The furniture was worn but comfortable. The rustic decor included many items made out of birch bark and logs. Old family photos littered the pine tables, and his grandmother's homey touches could be seen in the flow-blue china dishes displayed in the china cabinet and the quirky antique salt and pepper shaker collection that lined the kitchen windowsill. Even the old jadeite-green batter bowl that Gram used to let him lick her homemade cake batter from still sat on the stainless steel counter. The place was home.

The best part about it was that Gramps had had the

foresight to buy up twenty acres of land, so Sam didn't have a soul nearby. Nothing but deer and bears for company, just the way he liked it. He even owned a few acres across the street, where the land sloped down to reveal a pond. Sometimes at dusk the deer would come to the edges of the pond, and Sam would sit on the porch to watch them, just as he'd done with his dad and Gramps when he was a little boy.

Thorne had approached him about buying up part of the land, but Sam would never sell. Thorne would only get it over his dead body.

Sam brought the beer over to the little desk situated under the overhang of the loft. He cracked the small window on the wall next to the desk just an inch. The cool night air washed over him. In the woods, he heard the hoot of a barn owl and the reply of another.

He sipped his beer and thought about Jo. He admired the way she'd handled Jesse. In fact, she was probably one of the best cops he'd ever worked with. Funny thing, though, even though they'd been side by side every day for four years, he still felt as if he didn't *really* know her. Sure, they hung out sometimes and talked a lot at work, but there was something there, just below the surface, that he couldn't put a finger on. Something in her private life she wanted to keep private. Then again, who could blame her? Sam had some of that himself.

He fired up the computer and navigated to the financial site where he had his 401k just as his phone dinged.

He pulled it out of his pocket. His daughter, Hayley.

Hey Dad, just checking in. U keeping everyone honest up there?

Sam's heart expanded. One good thing had come from his first marriage—his twin daughters. He typed a reply.

Much as I can. How's school?

Hayley was studying at the Boston School of Pharmacology. Her twin sister, Marla, was studying marine biology, also in Massachusetts. He missed them both. They were too far away.

Semester almost over. Coming up to visit soon.

Sam replied:

Can't wait.

The phoned dinged again. Marla this time. Sam smiled. When one of them texted, the other was soon to follow. He exchanged a similar text conversation with Marla. He figured they'd come to visit at the same time. Sam made a mental note to make sure there were clean sheets for the guest room and loft.

Texting with his girls brought up thoughts of their mother, his first wife. Vanessa. They'd been high school sweethearts and had a volatile relationship. It had been both good and bad. In the end, it was mostly bad. Still, she'd had some sort of hold on him. Sam thought maybe she had a special place in his heart because she was the mother of his children. Whatever the reason, he could never refuse her anything. They'd tried to get back together a few times, but it never worked out. When she moved to Las Vegas, it had been a relief.

Thoughts of his daughters also reminded him of Dupont's threat. Had his words just been idle speculation, or did Dupont know more about what had happened during Sam's cousin Gracie's rape trial twenty years ago than Sam thought he did?

The rape had happened in Boston, and two of the rapists had been Harvard students, just like Dupont. But Dupont's name had never come up. He'd acted shocked and conciliatory back then. As far as Sam knew, Dupont hadn't even known them.

The trial had been splashed all over the papers, so Dupont knew enough just from that, but how much did he know about the part Sam and Mick had played in making sure justice prevailed?

Sam turned back to his computer. What did it matter what Dupont knew? He didn't regret what he'd done. Sometimes the system needed a little help to make sure justice prevailed and that people couldn't buy their way out of prosecution.

And sometimes you needed to skirt the system to make sure those that needed help the most got it. He clicked into his retirement account and withdrew a sizable chunk of money. He couldn't do anything to bring Tyler Richardson back to his family, but maybe this would help ease their pain.

CHAPTER NINE

S am was the first one into the station the next day and headed straight to the coffee machine. The K-Cup brewer was a new addition purchased by Reese, who had gotten sick of cleaning out the old coffee pot that they always seemed to burn the last of the coffee in. It was expensive, though, and not in the budget, so they all brought in their own K-Cups.

Sam picked up his orange K-Cup of Gorilla organic, popped it into the receptacle, and pressed the brew button. The smell of coffee wafted up.

He glanced at the rack where their K-Cups were all neatly stacked. Tea for Reese, dark roast for Jo, generic for Kevin. His eyes fell on the Moonbucks brand. Tyler's brand. A hollow feeling filled his stomach, and his eyes flicked automatically to the empty desk in the corner.

L A DOBBS

"Pop one in for me, will ya," Jo said then stopped short, following his gaze. Her face immediately softened, her eyes misting.

Sam turned his attention back to the coffeemaker. He removed his spent K-Cup and popped hers in, swapping his now-steaming blue police-issue mug for the bright-yellow smiley-face mug she preferred. When it was full, he handed it to her.

They proceeded to Jo's desk. She sat in the chair, her hands curled around the steaming mug. Sam rested his hip on the corner of her desk, and she offered him a jelly donut from the white bag she'd brought. Their usual morning routine. It was the closest thing to a meeting they ever had, crowded around Jo's desk, discussing their plan of attack for the day. Of course, there were usually three of them. The fact Tyler wasn't there weighed heavily on Sam, and judging by the way Jo kept glancing at the empty desk, he could tell it did on her too.

Sam was just about to start talking about the Palmer case when the door opened and Reese came in with the phone pressed to her ear.

"Yes, Mrs. Deardorff. I know that goats can be very destructive."

Reese shot a look at Sam and rolled her eyes. "Yes, I know Mrs. Hoelscher needs to keep Bitsy in her yard. No, we can't put a restraining order on a goat. I'll have an officer come by to take your statement."

"They're at it again, huh?" Jo asked.

Nettie Deardorff and Rita Hoelscher had been next-door neighbors for over fifty years. The two widows didn't have much to do but complain about each other. Sam didn't know what had happened to start it, but ever since he could remember, the two had been feuding. Lately, Nettie had been complaining about Rita's goat, Bitsy. The previous week, she'd complained Bitsy had eaten up all her bulbs from her garden. The only way to appease them was to send an officer out and pretend the other woman would get punished somehow.

"This time, she's saying Bitsy chewed her siding." Reese flipped a postcard to Sam.

"That's odd. She complained about Bitsy last week. I thought it was Nettie's turn this week," Jo said.

"Maybe they are getting senile and forgetting whose week it is," Reese said.

Jo eyed the postcard over her steaming mug. It had a big pink flamingo on the front. "What's that?"

Sam flipped it over and recognized the oversized shaky scrawl.

IT'S hot as hell down here. And boring. Only talk about knee replacements and gout. Get me out of here. P.S. Sorry about Tyler

. . .

-H

"IT'S FROM HARRY." Sam flipped the card to her, and she smiled. Harry Woolston was the former chief of police. Harry had held the job for what seemed like a hundred years. He hadn't wanted to retire, but age had forced him out. Now he was down in Florida and bored out of his mind.

The two months he came back in the summer, he usually spent pestering Sam for information on the various cases they were working. Though Sam had to admit his advice did come in handy sometimes. Harry was more old school than Sam and didn't believe in any of the newfangled methods of forensics. He refused to use a computer, and Sam didn't even know if he knew how.

Jo set the card aside. "I guess we better get back over to the campsite. Let them know we're dealing with a murder."

Sam figured rumor might have already gotten around to them, but he knew Jo wanted to watch them as he gave them the news. Maybe one of them would have some kind of a nervous tic or something that would give them away. Sam wished it would be so easy, but he knew it wouldn't.

"Yep. Kevin can take pictures. The ones I took yesterday are just on my phone. We need something better." Sam held up his phone. "And we can compare what Kevin takes to what I took to see if anybody moved anything."

"And we can find out why they lied about Jesse." Jo drained her mug.

"Maybe Jesse was the one that was lying."

"Good point. He was acting kinda cagey. He has a tic in his shoulder that gives him away. And he was scratching a bug bite, so I know he was in the woods. But I think he would've been more nervous if he was the killer. He seemed genuinely surprised about the murder, even if he is hiding something."

The door opened, and Kevin sauntered toward the coffee pot. "Hi, guys."

"Hey, Kevin. We're headed back to the campground today."

Kevin turned while his mug was filling. "Whole different line of questioning when you know it's a murder, right?"

"I was hoping you could take more pictures of the area where we found the clothes after you left yesterday. We think that might be the murder site." Sam saw Reese waving around some paperwork at her desk. "Oh, and I need you to head over to Nettie Deardorff's. She's complaining about Rita Hoelscher's goat again."

Kevin rolled his eyes. "Sure. Okay."

"I was wondering if you wanted to log a few extra hours. With this murder investigation and us being shorthanded..." Sam's voice trailed off, and everyone looked in the direction of Tyler's empty desk.

"I can put in a few extra, I suppose." Kevin turned back toward them, and something dark flashed in his narrowed eyes. "Is there anything new about the investigation?"

"We're not supposed to be investigating it," Jo said.

"Yeah, I know. But you guys are investigating it, aren't you?" Kevin's voice rose at the end. "I mean, we want to find out what happened to him, don't we?"

Sam glanced at Jo. Since Kevin was part time, they didn't work as closely together. Kevin was a good cop, but he didn't feel a connection with him like he had with Jo and Tyler. But Kevin was part of the team, and his help might come in handy. Jo nodded slightly.

"I've had Mick looking into a few things," Sam said. "The only lead we have is the stolen car. And so far we have no leads as to who took it."

"And the fingerprint we found on the ashtray," Jo added. "We ran it through AFIS, but nothing came up. Whoever it is isn't in the system."

Kevin made a face. "Weird that the staties' investigation hasn't turned anything up. I mean, why was he out there? Why hadn't he pulled his gun? What did his log say?"

Jo cleared her throat. "Well, he didn't exactly put it in the log."

Kevin's brows shot up. "What do you mean? We're

supposed to either call things in or log them in our notebook. And since it was after midnight and there was no one to call it in to..."

"Right. He should have written the stop in his notebook. But you know how it is when you're out there alone. He probably saw the car and was pulling over to help. I'm sure he didn't think it was going to be any police business," Jo said. "Probably figured he'd change the tire and send the motorist on his way."

"It's still supposed to be logged. Wouldn't that have been a red flag for the staties?" Kevin asked.

"Yeah, well, they didn't exactly know that he didn't log it." Jo took a deep breath. "I wrote the stop in his notebook the next day after he died."

"You *what*?" Kevin's voice rose. "If Dupont finds out, he'll have a field day with that."

Jo held up her palms. "I know. But I didn't want anything to tarnish Tyler's reputation. If they saw he didn't go strictly by the book, they might've tried to make it into something it wasn't." She shook her head at Kevin's incredulous look. "Come on. We all know that Tyler was a good guy. He was probably just trying to help, and you know none of us go one-hundred-percent by the book in writing this stuff down. We all do it at the end of the shift. I just did it for him because he couldn't do it for himself anymore."

The three of them stared at each other while Kevin

thought about it. Sam started to get nervous. Would Kevin tell Dupont?

After a few seconds, Kevin sighed. "Yeah, I suppose you're right." He slipped the rubber lid onto his travel mug and grabbed the digital camera off his desk. "You guys ready?"

CHAPTER TEN

The campers had told Sam the day before that they planned to extend their stay at the campground. They wanted to stick around until they knew exactly what had happened to Lynn. He reckoned at least some of them were going to be surprised by the news that Lynn's death had not been accidental. But was there one that wouldn't be?

When they arrived, Kevin headed straight to the spot where they'd found Lynn's clothes. Jo and Sam descended on the campsite.

The smell of bacon permeated the air, reminding Sam of dozens of camping trips he himself had enjoyed. At the picnic table, Noah was manning the Coleman stove. A pile of crisp bacon was stacked beside him on grease-soaked-paper-towel-lined plates.

A fire crackled inside the ring of rocks. A thick

metal grate covered the fire, and on top of that, a cast-iron skillet held fluffy yellow eggs. Lawn chairs sat haphazardly around the site. Bottles of vodka, rum, and Jack Daniels were lined up next to a stack of sixteen-ounce red plastic Solo cups on top of a large blue cooler.

The campers were busy either cooking or tidying up the site. Julie was folding colorful towels. Derek collected kindling, twigs snapping under his hiking boots as he scoured the woods at the edge of the site. Up in the trees, a squirrel chittered. Birds twittered. Beyond the campsite, the river rolled past.

A mosquito buzzed Sam, and he waited patiently for it to land on his arm. When it did, he smacked it flat, leaving only a smudge of brown and a dot of blood as evidence.

Everyone stopped what they were doing and turned to Jo and Sam. Their somber faces reflected a mixture of hope and fear.

Noah stepped forward, the large fork still in his hand. "Any news?"

Sam nodded slowly. "Afraid it's not good. Lynn didn't slip and fall. She was murdered, and then her body was put in the river."

"*Murdered?*" Joshua's eyes widened.

The looks of shock on their faces seemed genuine. The women started crying.

Noah scrubbed his hands across his face. "I don't

understand. Who would kill Lynn?" He looked around at his group of friends. No one had an answer.

"That's what we need to find out," Sam said. "Did she have any jealous boyfriends? Any enemies?"

Julie stepped up. "We're her closest friends. I don't know of anyone that would want to harm Lynn." She looked at the others, her face falling. "Do you guys?"

They shook their heads.

"What about that guy from the bar?" Tara said. "We don't know anything about him. He could be a killer."

"We talked to him last night," Jo said. She had her polarized Oakley Standard Issue sunglasses on and her hair stuffed under a navy-blue cap with WRPD stamped in white letters on the front. "He denied even being here."

"He's lying." Noah's voice rose in anger. "He was here. And the people from the other campsite were here, too. It could have been one of them. It couldn't be anyone that knew her."

"We'll look into it. But I want you guys to think hard if you know of any reason that someone would want to harm her. Was anyone angry with her?" Sam's gaze drifted around the group. "Maybe someone close to her that had a grudge?"

Derek's hands curled into fists, and he moved closer to Sam. "Now wait a minute. Are you saying it was one of us?"

Josh stepped in next to him. "Why aren't you

looking into that guy from the bar instead of accusing us? Is it because he's a local?"

Sam held up his hands, his voice gentle. "We're looking into everyone. I'm not accusing any of you, but since you knew her best, you'd be the ones to know if anyone might have had a reason to want her out of the way."

That seemed to mollify them, and both Josh and Derek relaxed their stance.

"In the meantime, we're going to need to take her things," Sam said. "There could be a clue in there."

Everyone glanced toward the red tent, frozen on their spot, then finally Julie broke from the group. "I'll break things down for you."

Jo already had the latex gloves on. "I'll do it. It's important that we don't contaminate it."

Julie's eyes filled, and her lower lip quivered. She nodded and stepped back while Jo got to work.

Twenty minutes later, they were in the Tahoe with Julie's tent and her duffel bag full of clothes. A few miles down the road, Sam saw the giant coffee cup of the Brewed Awakening coffee shop. The K-Cup coffee at the station was okay, but there was nothing better than a fresh brew from Brewed Awakening.

"Coffee?" Sam asked.

Jo made a face. "You have to ask?"

He signaled for the right turn, and just before he started to turn in, a candy-apple-red Cadillac swooped in front of him, cutting them off and making Sam slam on the brakes. Sam laid on the horn, but the man in the car simply turned an arrogant face to them, smiled, and waved.

"Thorne." Jo spat out the name.

As Sam drove forward toward the drive-through, Jo twisted in her seat, looking over her sunglasses at Thorne as he parked, taking up two spots. Thorne got out of the car. He was in his late forties, still in good shape but with a bit of thickening around his middle. His hair was dyed black, and he walked with the self-important air of someone who is used to getting his way.

"He looks so smug. We should arrest him for driving to endanger." Jo turned to face forward and pushed the sunglasses back up on her nose.

"Be more trouble than it's worth."

They ordered coffees in Styrofoam cups, and Jo bought her usual half-dozen jelly donuts. Sam had no idea where she put all the donuts she ate. Even with her bulky police belt, she was trim. He could never eat that many donuts. Since he'd turned forty, he'd noticed his pants fitting a little tighter. The only solution was to cut down on food and beer. Jo hadn't seemed to cut down any since he'd known her. She wasn't much younger, but maybe she had a fast metabolism. Some people were just lucky that way.

"So, what do you think about the friends?" Jo fished

a jelly donut out of the bag. "Do you think it could be one of them?"

"I don't know. They seemed genuinely surprised. I'll have Reese check into their backgrounds, but there doesn't seem to be any connection. And this murder was definitely done by someone who had a connection. What do you think?"

"I'm not so sure. They seemed nervous, like they were hiding something. Too quick to try to blame someone else."

"Natural reaction. No one wants to think their friends are capable of murder."

Jo bit into the donut, and a blob of jelly squirted onto her finger. She licked it off. "What about Jesse? I saw him scratching a bug bite last night. He probably *was* at the campground even though he said no. Which means he lied. I mean, I know he's not a pillar of society, but murder?"

"He could have gotten a bug bite anywhere." White Rock was loaded with wilderness, and the bugs could be persistent even in the middle of town. "I know what you mean, though. Seems like Lynn's friends would be pretty dumb to lie about Jesse being there. Too easy to prove them wrong. And most of them agreed he was there, so unless they were all in on it, I think it's a good bet he *was* there. But why would Jesse lie?"

Finished with the donut, Jo flipped the plastic tab on her lid and sipped the coffee. "Who knows with him.

Probably didn't want to get into trouble and denied it as his first reaction. Maybe he isn't smart enough to figure out we'd catch him. Unless there is more going on with him that we don't know about."

"I guess I'll be paying him a visit," Sam said. "In the meantime, we need to find out more about Lynn's finances. I know the company isn't doing well, but she has a stake in it. That stake might be worth something after this new game is released. Which makes me wonder exactly who would benefit from that in the event of her death."

CHAPTER ELEVEN

S am dropped Jo at the station and headed to Riddell's Auto Body, where Jesse worked, finishing off his coffee on the way. His stomach growled. Maybe he should have grabbed one of those jelly donuts.

He parked in the dirt lot and casually walked into the shop.

The waiting room was open to the service area, and he could hear the clank of metal tools and smell the grease and engine oil. Three people sat in the waiting room, bored looks on their faces as they stared at the syndicated talk show that played on the TV in the corner. Jesse was in bay number three, working on securing the lug nuts of a tire.

He looked up as Sam approached, a frown creasing his forehead. He stood. His navy-blue coveralls were smeared with grease, and judging by the look on his face, Sam knew he'd guessed he wasn't there for an oil change.

"Hey, man, I'm at work here." Jesse glanced around nervously.

Sam had picked his workplace on purpose, knowing Jesse wouldn't be able to walk away from him. Not only that, but Sam was friends with the owner. He glanced over at the fat, balding man. "Hey, Al, you mind if I have a word with Jesse?"

Al's dark eyes were expressionless as he shook his head.

Sam jerked his head toward the back door, and Jesse wiped his hands on the front of his coveralls, adding a new grease smear in the process.

The landscaping in back of the shop consisted of a patch of dry dirt ringed with weeds. Jesse leaned against the thickly painted off-white cinderblock wall and stuffed his hands in his pockets. He was trying to act casual, but Sam could see he was nervous.

"If this is about that camping girl, I didn't have anything to do with it. I told you I wasn't there," Jesse said.

"Really? I've got half the campground that says you were."

Jesse looked down and dug at the dirt with the toe of a scuffed black work boot. "I wasn't at *their* campsite."

So he *had* been lying. Sam had a good idea why. He knew a lot about what went on in town. He didn't always act on what he knew, which made some people assume that he wasn't clued in. Sam didn't mind that at all. In fact, he preferred it when people underestimated him. It made them act sloppy, and when people acted sloppy, they made mistakes. Sam knew that Jesse had recently started dealing pot, and his guess was that was what he had been doing at the campground.

Sam figured Jesse had lied because he didn't want to get caught selling pot. It was still illegal in New Hampshire. But Sam couldn't give a crap about that—next to catching a murderer, nailing someone for selling pot was way down on his list.

Sam thought about his suspicions that Thorne was the reason for the uptick in drugs in the area. Not just pot—it was much worse. Meth, heroin, cocaine. One minor pot dealer was nothing compared to catching the guy at the top of the chain. Much better to keep on friendly terms with Jesse. That alliance might come in handy later.

Sam leaned against the wall close to Jesse. He was taller by about five inches and used the intimidating size difference to his advantage. "But you *were* at the campground. And rumor has it you were doing a little business there."

Jesse's eyes darted around like a scared rabbit's, looking anywhere but Sam's face. "Look, I don't want to get in trouble. I don't know anything about that girl."

"Jesse, do you know what the sentence is for selling marijuana?"

Jesse's shoulders slumped, and all the wind whooshed out of him. Turned out he wasn't as tough as he liked to pretend. He caved easily. "I don't normally sell it. It's not like I'm a big dealer or anything. I just needed some extra money."

"Where'd you get it?"

"I don't know."

Sam lowered his voice and spoke slowly and steadily. He looked him dead in the eye. "You don't know? I'm not buying that, Jesse, and neither will the judge."

Sam paused for a few seconds to let his words sink in then added, "But I might be willing to make you a deal if you tell me the truth about what happened last night."

Jesse looked suspicious. "What kind of deal?"

"I won't breathe a word about your illegal extracurricular activities. In fact, unless you have any on you right now, I'm going to forget all about it."

Jesse spread his hands. Not so tough now. "I don't have any on me. I swear."

Sam simply waited.

"Okay. I was there last night. I'd seen her in the bar. She was cute. And we struck up a conversation. I met her friends, and I mentioned I had some weed, and they invited me back after the bar closed. But all we did was drink and smoke a few joints, and then I left. I swear she was alive when I left."

"Can anyone verify this?" Sam asked.

"Well, yeah, all the people at the campsite. I only stayed for about an hour and then went home."

"You didn't go anywhere else or see anyone?"

Jesse thought a minute. "I stopped to get gas at Cumbies then went straight home. Brian, my roommate, was already in bed."

"When you were at the campsite, did you see anything unusual? Was anybody angry with Lynn, or did anyone act funny around her?"

Jesse thought for a minute. "Come to think of it, I did see something. Not at the campsite. When we were in the bar. There was a blonde with them. She was kinda cute too, but she was with one of the guys. I saw her follow that girl, Lynn, to the ladies' room, and when I went down the hallway to the men's room shortly thereafter, I heard them in there having a rip-roaring argument."

"What were they arguing about?"

"I have no idea, but they must've made up. They didn't argue at the campsite." Jesse eyed Sam cautiously. "So do we have a deal?"

Sam studied him for a minute and then nodded.

Relief spread across Jesse's face. "Good, now I gotta get back to work."

Jesse turned and went inside the building.

Sam smiled. He had Jesse right where he wanted him now. He'd done Jesse a favor. So now if Sam got more evidence that Thorne really was involved in all the drugs coming into town, maybe Jesse would see his way to returning that favor by letting Sam know who he had gotten the drugs from. That person might be the next step in proving that Thorne was the source.

Not only that, but he had another lead to check out in the murder of Lynn Palmer.

CHAPTER TWELVE

J o leaned back in her chair. She had a half-eaten donut on her desk and her foot propped up on an overturned trash can. She tapped a staccato rhythm with the end of her pencil as she stared at the photos arranged on the big corkboard on the wall beside the window. She'd meticulously gone through Lynn's things, photographing each item and then putting them in an evidence box.

Near as she could tell, it was all normal stuff any camper would have. Lynn's belongings were practical, each item labeled inconspicuously with her initials. Nothing fancy. Even her undergarments were sensible. Plain white cotton with a tiny pink bow as the only ornamentation. It was a brand Jo wore herself—Plain Jane. It was known for the high-quality non-frilly designs. One thing was odd—no purse or cell phone.

She could see not bringing a purse on a camping trip, and Lynn's seemingly practical nature made it plausible, but a cell phone? Didn't everyone have those at all times these days?

Over at the receptionist desk, Reese was taking care of the usual day's business. In a small-town police station, you had to wear a lot of hats, and Reese handled most of the administrative activities. Dog licenses, collecting tax and sewer bills, issuing permits. Right now, she was issuing a yard-sale permit to Bev Porterfield.

"No, Mrs. Porterfield. You can't sell your husband."

"Why not? He's about as useful as that old 8-track player I found in the garage. I'm putting that out for sale."

"I'm sure you'd miss him if someone snapped him up. You wouldn't want Dottie Aldrich to get him, would you?"

Jo couldn't see Bev from where she sat, but she almost laughed out loud picturing the look that must have been on Bev's face as she thought about her husband hooking up with Dottie. Dottie was known as somewhat of a gold digger in the senior-citizen circles.

Reese continued, "Anyway, I don't really need to know the exact items you are going to sell to issue the permit. I just need the dates."

"You sure? I'm going to have a lot of old clothes and some antiques from my mother. In fact, I'm going to have her old china set, and the bassinet from Louis and..."

Jo tuned Bev Porterfield's words out as she listed a plethora of items she would have at her yard sale. Jo could just picture Reese rolling her eyes. She let it turn into background noise as her mind tossed around the various scenarios that could have led to Lynn Palmer's death.

Her thoughts turned to Lynn's friends at the camp-site. Most of them were definitely showing signs of hiding something. It could be that they were just nervous. Even innocent people got that way when a close friend was murdered. But Jo had a feeling that some of them, especially Noah, weren't telling the whole truth. The best bet was to separate them and talk to them individually—that was when the truth usually came out.

Her gaze drifted to the window. The maple and oak trees were sprouting fresh new green leaves. Birds hopped from branch to branch, swooping to the ground to grab up an occasional seed from the grass. In the distance, layers of hazy blue mountains contrasted with the white spire of the church at the end of Main Street. It was an idyllic small-town scene.

Ruining the pleasant scene, however, was Mayor Dupont striding down the sidewalk and into the town's one fine-dining establishment, Lago. Nothing but the best for the mayor.

He stopped at the door, plastering a fake smile on his face and greeting someone walking down the sidewalk. The smile dropped from his lips as the person passed, and he opened the door and pushed his way inside, cutting off a tourist who had been angling for the restaurant. Typical.

What wasn't typical was what she saw right after that. The cherry-red Cadillac pulled to the curb, and Lucas Thorne stepped out. He checked his watch—a Rolex, she knew from dealing with him previously—looked toward the town offices, and then glanced into the restaurant before darting inside.

Was he meeting with Dupont? Or was her imagination just on overdrive? The restaurant was public, so even if they were meeting, they weren't trying to hide it, so it was probably nothing nefarious.

She was still staring at the door when a third surprise happened. The door opened, and Kevin walked out.

Had Kevin been lunching at Lago? Expensive on the salary of a part-time cop. But maybe he could afford it. Jo suspected that Kevin had family money. She'd been to his house once. The unassuming small cape had been upgraded with the finest trappings. Granite countertops, cherry cabinets, bamboo flooring, and all the electronic gadgets one could wish for. Maybe that was why Kevin never seemed to want to take on more hours. If he had family money, he probably didn't even need a job.

"Oh no!" Reese's distraught voice pulled her attention from the window, and she swung around, planting her feet on the floor. She peered through the glass slats of the post-office-box partition. Bev Porterfield must have left, and Reese was alone at her desk, staring down at her computer, her dark hair hanging down the side of her face like a curtain.

"What's wrong?"

"Eric just emailed me. Lucy ran away."

"Maybe she ran home to her family." Jo's words ended a hopeful octave higher than they started.

"I don't think so," Reese said. "Eric said he doubted she even had one. I mean, you saw the condition she was in. Nobody was taking good care of her."

A pang of regret speared Jo. She hated to think of the dog out on the streets. Maybe she should've taken her in. Another living, breathing creature to come home to might be nice. But her landlord had been adamant about the no-pets rule. Maybe she should think about buying a place where she could actually have a dog. Maybe it was time she admitted that she actually wanted to put down roots here in White Rock.

"In happier news, I was able to find out something interesting about Lynn Palmer pertaining to her company, Lyah."

"You did? How did you do that?"

Reese scooted her chair around the partition. Her laptop was in her lap, and she had one faded-jean-clad leg curled under her, the other used for scooting.

"I have my ways," she teased.

Jo frowned. "Legal ways?"

There might've been times when they pushed the envelope, but if they wanted things to be admissible in court, Jo had to make sure that there was no way a defense attorney could have any evidence thrown out. If Reese had hacked into some computer files, they wouldn't be admissible in court. Jo suspected Reese was even more skilled in computer forensics than she'd let on to either her or Sam.

Reese held up her hands. "Totally legal. I simply called her lawyer and asked."

Jo held the white donut bag from Brewed Awakening out, and Reese took one. There were only two left. Had Jo eaten the rest? She didn't remember—she'd been so focused on the case.

"How did you find out who her lawyer was?"

"Does that part have to be legal? I mean, one could get that information from anywhere. Her friends. Her parents. We wouldn't have to prove how we found out who he is, right?" Reese bit into the donut, some of the sugar sprinkling down on the keyboard. She brushed it off and grabbed a napkin out of the bag.

Jo thought about that. As long as the information was gathered legally, who would know how she found out who the lawyer was? She made a mental note to ask about the lawyer in some official capacity so as to cover their asses. "You might be right. What did you find out?"

"Lynn and Noah used to be an item. They started that company together. The name, Lyah, is actually a mashup of their first names. They wanted to make sure the other could maintain control if something happened, so there's a codicil in Lynn's will that says her stock shares go to Noah in the event of her death. He has one leaving his shares to her, supposedly."

Jo leaned back in the chair and clasped her hands together, her elbows on the arms of her chair. "Now, that is interesting."

Kevin came around the post-office-box partition. "You guys found something interesting?"

"Reese discovered that Lynn Palmer's will lists Noah as a beneficiary of her interests in the company. Did you stop for lunch?" Jo said.

"Huh?" Kevin frowned at her. "Oh, no." He held up the camera. "I was out taking pictures. Just got back from the campground." He looked at his watch. "In fact, I think I may have worked more hours than I'm supposed to. I don't know what the budget is for extra hours, do you?"

Jo shook her head. That was Sam's area.

Kevin handed her the camera. "You can tell Sam all the pictures are on here."

"Okay." Jo watched him leave. Weird that he said he wasn't at lunch when she'd seen him coming out of the restaurant. What had he been doing in there?

She'd never clicked with Kevin, not like she did with Sam and Tyler, but still, she had no good reason to think ill of him. She'd learned over the years that she had to rein in her instincts to be suspicious of everyone. Just because bad things had happened in her past, it didn't mean everyone was out to get her.

There were plenty of reasons for Kevin to be in Lago. Maybe he knew someone that worked there. Maybe he was following up on something else. Maybe he was handing them his resume. Jo wouldn't be too disappointed if it was the latter, other than the fact it would mean they were even more short-handed.

She was staring out the window at the disappearing taillights of Kevin's Isuzu when Sam's Tahoe came around the corner and pulled up to the curb.

CHAPTER THIRTEEN

A s Sam parked the Tahoe, a blurry black-and-tan
movement at the side of the building behind the
shrubs caught his eye. He got out of the truck, and a
furry ball shot toward him. Lucy.

"What are you doing here?" He bent down and
petted the dog. Had her family claimed her, and were
they bringing her downtown? He doubted it—she had
no collar or leash.

He headed toward the front door, Lucy on his heels.
Sam stood with his hand on the oversized brass handle
and looked down at her. "You can't come in."

As soon as one of the double oak doors was cracked
open, Lucy shoved her nose through the opening and
pushed her way inside. So much for the dog listening
to him.

"Lucy!" Reese scooted her chair across the room and swirled to a stop in front of Lucy. Lucy wagged her tail profusely while Reese lavished her with attention. Reese cocked her head and looked inquisitively up at Sam. "What's she doing with you?"

"She was outside when I pulled up. I was going to ask you why she was here."

Reese shook her head. "I don't know. Eric said she ran away. She must've come here. Maybe she thinks this is home."

Sam's heart sank. No one had claimed the dog.

"Looks like she wants to be a police dog," Jo said.

"Yeah, don't tell Dupont. Unfortunately, having a K-9 unit costs money. She has to go back to the shelter. She looks good all cleaned up, though. I'm sure someone will adopt her if she doesn't have a family." Sam tried to ignore the pleading look in Lucy's whiskey-colored eyes. There was no budget for a police dog, and he couldn't have her at home.

He'd gotten used to living alone. He didn't want another person. But a dog was another story. Dogs didn't argue with you or talk back. Dogs were always happy to see you no matter what you'd done the day before.

But his days stretched out too long. He knew Dupont would balk if he tried to have her in the Tahoe, so he would be forced to leave her at home alone. And sometimes his day stretched out to fourteen hours or more. Heck, sometimes he didn't even go home at all. Now that they were shorthanded, he'd be at work even more. It wouldn't be fair to Lucy. She deserved better than that.

Reese's smile faded. "I know. I'll call Eric."

Jo grabbed the donut bag from the corner of her desk. Lucy's ears perked up at the crinkle of the paper.

"Can dogs eat donuts?" Jo asked.

Reese made a face and patted her stomach. "Desserts aren't good for them just like they're not good for us."

Lucy thumped her tail and whined, her eyes fixated on the donut that Jo was now holding up.

"I suppose a tiny piece wouldn't hurt," Reese said.

Jo broke off a piece and flipped it to Lucy, who leapt up in the air and caught it in her mouth.

"Pretty good catch." Sam rubbed Lucy's ears then noticed the photographs laid out on the corkboard. His mind immediately went into investigation mode. "Are those the items from Lynn Palmer's tent?"

Jo put the bag down and went to stand at the board. "Yep. Pretty standard stuff for campers." She pointed to the pictures in turn. "Rain gear, jeans, undergarments, sweats, hiking shorts."

"Nothing out of the ordinary," Sam said. His eyes were still on the items, his mind inventorying each piece for later use.

"No. Except." Jo drew out the word as she turned

around and pointed to one of the photos. It was a pair of cotton pants ripped on the side. "This is from the pile of clothes we found in the woods. The pants were ripped as if they snagged on something or there was a struggle."

"Or maybe she was in a hurry to get them off."

"If that were the case, would she have taken the time to fold them in a neat pile?" Jo tapped her index finger on the photo Sam had taken of the clothing pile. "The other unusual thing is that I didn't find a cell phone."

"Maybe it wasn't in her tent. It could still be lying around at the campsite."

Jo nodded. "It'd be important to get it. You never know when that last text or phone call is going to provide a clue. Speaking of which, what did you find out from Jesse?"

Sam plopped into a chair and leaned forward, his elbows on his knees. He absently stroked the soft fur on Lucy's head as he told Jo what he'd gleaned from Jesse. He left out the part about the pot—not that he didn't trust Jo, but the fewer people that knew, the better. He didn't want word getting out that he let criminals off the hook, but sometimes you had to let the smaller fish go in order to catch the bigger one.

"That must be Amber she fought with. Do you think Amber had something to do with her death? Maybe killed her from jealousy?" Jo pressed her lips together. "She did seem awfully possessive of Noah. Maybe they had a fight about Noah and Lynn was killed in a jealous rage? That's interesting, because I have a theory too, thanks to Reese."

Jo and Reese took turns telling Sam about Lynn's will. He was getting a new appreciation for Reese's computer skills. She had a knack for digging up information, though he suspected she pushed the envelope sometimes.

"Noah was angry at the campsite. Almost too angry," Jo said. "Sometimes people act that way when they have something to hide, so—"

"*Woof!*"

They spun around to see Dupont standing in the lobby on the other side of the post-office boxes. Lucy had wandered over to the partition and was standing there glaring at him. The hairs along her spine were raised like a mohawk.

"What is this dog doing here? I thought I told you people to get rid of it," Dupont demanded.

Lucy must not have liked being called "it." She kept her eyes trained on Dupont and resorted to a low growl.

Reese rushed to Lucy's side. "We brought her to the shelter, but she must've run off. I'll bring her back as soon as I can."

Dupont looked at Reese dubiously. "Make it soon. We can't have an animal like that in a public office. Do you see the way she growled at me? What if she bit a kid or something? Would make me look like a shoddy mayor."

"Wouldn't want that." Reese's voice had a tinge of sarcasm that made Dupont look at her twice. She ignored him and pushed Lucy behind her desk.

Dupont proceeded into the squad room. Sam stood as the man approached. He didn't need Dupont looking down on him. Sam was taller, and he figured it was better to have it the other way around.

"I don't think I need to remind you who has control of the budget here." Dupont's eyes flicked to Tyler's empty desk, and Sam felt that familiar hollow sinking sensation.

"I know you lost a good man." Dupont's face softened. For a second, he seemed almost human. "I'm willing to keep the third full-time officer in the budget, but you people need to produce results. What's going on in the Palmer case?"

"We were just discussing that." Sam pointed to the corkboard. "We have a few suspects, and we're going to continue questioning. If you would just let us do our job instead of coming in here and bugging us, we could have it solved sooner."

Dupont scowled, and Sam could practically feel Jo suppressing a smirk behind him. She usually remained quiet when Dupont was around, mostly because if she opened her mouth, whatever came out typically wasn't helpful.

"It was one of those hooligan friends of hers, wasn't it?" Dupont asked. "The parents have driven up and are very anxious and heartbroken over this."

An ache of sympathy bloomed in Sam's chest as he thought of how he would feel if one of his daughters had been murdered. He would be burning for justice. Sam wanted to do right by Lynn Palmer and her family. He couldn't give a crap about what Dupont wanted, but if they happened to be the same thing, then so be it.

"We understand that," Sam said. "We're working to get it solved as quickly as we can. Where are they staying? I could go talk to them. They might know something that could be helpful."

"I put them up at the Covered Bridge over on Route 11," Dupont said. "I want all hands on this. There's extra in the budget from the salary of Richardson. I strongly suggest you bring your part-time man up to full time and speed up the timeline of this case."

Sam glanced over at Kevin's desk. Unlike Sam's and Jo's messy desks, it was stacked neatly with papers, pencils, and a notebook. Kevin wasn't much of a go-getter, though he was an adequate cop. Sam didn't know if increasing his hours would help, but maybe they could have him work on the smaller local calls, freeing them up for more investigative work. "I'll do that."

Dupont gave a curt nod. He glowered at Sam and Jo then shot a parting look at Lucy on his way out.

"Sheesh. The guy acts like we're just lollygagging around, not trying to solve the case. Doesn't he know we want to solve it as much as anyone?" Jo asked.

"He just likes to be a pain in the ass. Where is Kevin, by the way?"

Jo handed him the digital camera. "He signed out. Said he was afraid he'd already worked too many hours. Pictures of the area where we found Lynn's clothes are in the camera."

"Okay, I guess I'll talk to him tomorrow about moving to full time."

Jo glanced at Tyler's desk. "Temporarily or for good?"

Sam sighed. "I guess we should offer him the position for good. I mean, it's only right. He's been here over a year now, and it would be the right thing to promote him."

Sam was all about doing the right thing, but for some reason, the hollow feeling in his chest told him he didn't really want Kevin as a replacement for Tyler.

"Yeah, I guess so." The tone of resignation in Jo's voice told him she was as enthusiastic about bringing Kevin to full time as he was.

"In the meantime, I say we waste no time in finding

out what the deal is with these suspects. Seems like Noah and Amber both might've had a reason to want Lynn out of the way. I say we question all the campers separately and see if we can find out what really happened the night Lynn Palmer was murdered."

CHAPTER FOURTEEN

J o was eager to see how the campers reacted to their visit. In her experience, the deeper you delved in an investigation, the more nervous people got, and the more nervous they got, the more apt they were to slip up. She shoved her yellow smiley mug under the coffee machine's spout and grabbed the little red K-Cup with the extra-caffeinated grounds. She could use the extra caffeine to keep her brain sharp so she'd be able to notice any telltale signs that their suspects were lying.

She balanced the warm mug in her hands from the passenger seat of the Tahoe as Sam drove them to the campsite.

They usually drove together like this when there wasn't much going on. They did a lot of their collaborating in the car on the way to talk to suspects or visit crime scenes. Somehow, the scenery of the mountains and the absence of traffic on the backcountry roads had a way of helping Jo think better.

"Thing is, they've already had over twenty-four hours to get their stories straight and try to cover their tracks," Sam said.

"I know. That's a bummer. But killers always make mistakes. If one of these kids killed her, they're bound to reveal themselves." Jo sipped the coffee. "But I don't think we should let on that we think one of them might have done it. We need to act friendly and see if we can get her cell phone. Once they realize we're treating them as suspects, they won't be so eager to comply with us."

"I want to check out the murder site again and the place where we found her clothes. Now that we know it's a murder, I need to look closer. You're right about not tipping them off to our suspicions. I'm going to make it seem like Jesse is our main suspect. I don't think he did it. Doesn't make sense for him. He has no motive unless it was a fit of anger because she rejected him when he came on to her. Jesse doesn't seem the fit-of-anger type. He didn't get that mad when I came to his work to interrogate him," Sam said.

Jo agreed. "We've never had any calls about him fighting. He's more the sneaky breaking-in-and-selling-weed type."

"I still want to double-check what he told me,

though. I would think one of them would've noticed that Lynn was still alive when Jesse left... *if* what he told me is the truth."

"Even if one of them did, they might lie if they are trying to point the finger away from them and toward Jesse."

"Playing along like we think it's Jesse will set them off guard and give us a chance to observe them before they realize what we're up to." Sam pulled into the campground, and the Tahoe bumped down the rutted path to the site. "It's late afternoon. I figure we'll start cutting them from the herd and getting down to business first thing tomorrow. Make it look like we're just asking them in for official statements."

They pulled up to the site. Jo set her mug in the cup holder. The base was a little too wide, but she'd found she could balance it at an angle on the top indentation and the mug wouldn't tip over. Usually.

Sam frowned at the precariously balanced cup, then his eyes moved to her navy-blue short-sleeved button-up shirt. "You have some jelly on your shirt."

Jo looked down to see a shiny red blob just below the white, gold, and light-blue police patch. "Darn it." She swiped at the blob, but it only smudged it in deeper.

Sam had already gotten out and was standing in the middle of the campsite. The campers surrounded him, their faces full of curiosity. Jo stood back and studied them. Was one of them a murderer? If so, she couldn't tell which one.

"Did you catch him?" a teary-eyed Tara was asking. She was holding a newer-model expensive backpack that Jo knew was supposed to be very lightweight. These folks really took their camping seriously.

"Not quite yet. We think she was killed over there." Sam nodded toward the area where they found the clothing. It was cordoned off with yellow crime scene tape strung between the pine trees. "And I want to take a better look to see if there's any evidence."

"What kind of evidence?" Joshua asked, his eyes drifting over to the area.

"Signs of a struggle, blood. If we had a big forensics team, they'd be combing the area, but we gotta work with what we have."

"What about that local guy?" Noah asked. "Did you bring him in?"

"We've had him in for questioning. In fact, I was wondering if you guys could verify something he told me." Sam started toward the area, and the crowd followed. Jo admired the way he was handling it. Totally nonconfrontational, as if he were taking them into his confidence as though they were allies in the investigation.

Sam slipped under the yellow tape and started to walk slowly around the area, his eyes fixed on the ground. The others stayed back behind the tape, probably conditioned to act that way after viewing a billion crime shows on TV.

"Jesse." Sam stopped his pacing and looked back at the crowd. "That's the guy from town who was here partying with you." Sam walked to the place where they'd found the pile of clothing. Sam had marked it with a birch stick the other day, and Kevin had come back and put a yellow police marker on the spot.

Sam crouched down, pushing leaves aside. The campers watched him quietly while they waited for him to continue.

"Anyway, Jesse said he was only here for an hour. Said Lynn was alive when he left." Sam stood up and looked at them again. "I was wondering if anyone here could verify that. Does anyone remember talking to Lynn after Jesse left?"

The campers exchanged looks. Jo watch them carefully. Most of them had blank faces as if they were trying to remember. Sam continued his search, making his way down to the beach, which was about twenty feet from the area where they'd found the clothes.

Jo slipped under the crime scene tape but stayed close to the campers. She made a show of sweeping the ground for clues while also keeping one eye on the campers.

"I don't think he *was* here. Lynn disappeared, and I don't remember seeing him after that." Tara raised her voice so Sam could hear. She looked at Josh. "Do you?"

"I don't know. We were all kind of drunk," Josh said. "I thought Lynn was in her tent."

Sam made his way back from the beach and slipped under the yellow crime scene tape, joining the campers on the campsite side. "Speaking of that, we didn't find her cell phone or a purse in her tent. Did she have them?"

Julie shook her head. "Not a purse. No sense in taking a purse camping. But she had a cell phone. Even though we're taking a few days off, we still need to be in contact with the people back at the office. We all brought our phones." As if to illustrate, she undid the flap on the side pocket of her khaki cargo pants and pulled out her phone.

Sam paced around the site. He inspected the picnic table and various chairs around the campsite. He didn't find a cell phone.

Sam was incredibly observant, and Jo figured he was taking mental notes of everything around the campsite. But it didn't take someone with Sam's skills to see there was no cell phone lying around.

"So where is it?" Jo asked as she slipped back under the yellow tape.

More blank looks were exchanged. Finally, Julie said, "Maybe it was in the woods near her clothes?"

Sam shook his head. "I just looked all around there, and I didn't come up with it. Have any of you found an extra cell phone?"

They shook their heads.

"Maybe that local guy from town took it for some reason," Amber suggested, looking to Noah for approval.

"Why would he do that?" Sam asked.

Her pretty forehead creased. "Well, I don't know, but it's missing."

"And none of you remember seeing Lynn alive after he left? When did he leave? I mean, it doesn't make sense that he'd kill her and then come back to the party, right? So he must've left after he killed her. *If* he did kill her."

More silence.

Then Noah said, "We weren't exactly looking at our watches every minute. We were having a party."

"What time did she die?" Tara asked.

Jo had been waiting for this. They purposely hadn't let out the time of death. They preferred to keep that close to the vest so the killer wouldn't have time to invent an alibi. But since it had been at 2:30 in the morning, she didn't know how useful that would be in this case. Most would claim they were in their tents sleeping.

"What time did your party end?" Sam asked as the phone in his pocket chirped. He pulled it out and glanced at the screen. "Gotta take this."

He stepped away, and Jo continued the questioning.

"Did anyone notice the time?" Jo asked.

Josh shrugged. "Like Noah said, we were partying, not clock watching."

"Wait a minute. We were at the bar till one. Then we came back here..." Julie's face was scrunched up as if she were trying to recall the sequence of events. "That guy, Jesse, followed us. He sold us... I mean we had a few drinks, and then we all started making our way to bed. We were going hiking the next day. Couldn't have been more than an hour after one."

"And Jesse was still there when you went to bed?" Jo asked.

Julie twisted her lips together. "I don't remember. Does anyone remember?"

Nobody did. Or if they did, they weren't saying.

Sam snapped the phone shut and came back to the group. "Okay. We have another call. Maybe you folks need a little time to think. I'd like you all to come to the station tomorrow so we can get official statements." At their looks of concern, he held up his hands. "Just standard procedure. We want to get to the bottom of this as much as you do. Officer Deckard has your phone numbers from the other day, and we'll be calling to let you know what time we want to talk to you. In the meantime, could you please look for Lynn's phone? It's important."

They promised to look, and Sam and Jo got into the Tahoe.

Jo picked up her mug. The coffee was lukewarm

now, but lukewarm was better than nothing. She was curious as to why Sam wasn't taking them in right away. Maybe he figured if he gave the killer enough rope, they'd hang themselves. "You giving them some time to think things over, or to get their story straight?"

"Neither. We have business. Being shorthanded really does put a crimp in the investigation."

"We got another call?"

Sam held up his phone. "Several. We got a cat up a tree on Cross Street, a fender bender on the corner of Owings and Main, and an altercation over at the Laundromat. The interrogations will have to wait until tomorrow. Maybe by then we'll be able to rule out one of our suspects."

"Really? Which one?"

"Jesse. He said he stopped for gas on the way home that night, and I have Ernie looking for the receipt. According to the campers, and Jesse's own account, he got there after the bar closed at one and left shortly after. That's a small time frame, and not too many people would have been stopping at the gas station that early in the morning. If Jesse paid with a credit card, all the better. We know Lynn was killed between two-thirty and three. Maybe the receipt will prove Jesse couldn't have done it."

Jo looked out the window. "I think we already know he didn't do it. We just need to figure out who did."

"Yep. Getting her phone would help. Do you think

she could have dropped it in the woods? Maybe we should start a grid search."

Jo took another lukewarm sip. The coffee had turned bitter, and she forced it down her throat. She didn't think they were going to find the phone in the woods. "I think a search would be a waste. My guess is someone took it. I think there's something on that phone the killer doesn't want us to see."

CHAPTER FIFTEEN

J o and Sam flipped a coin for the calls. She'd lost and had spent forty-five minutes at the Laundromat, settling an argument between Lola Ehrsam and Judith Crawford because Lola had taken Judith's clothes out of the dryer prematurely. Lola claimed it wasn't so, Judith hadn't put enough quarters in for a full cycle, and the machine was sitting there useless. Jo settled the dispute by buying both the women coffee and making Lola promise to fold Judith's clothes once they ran through the full cycle.

When she was done, Sam had rescued the cat from the tree and smoothed over things at the fender-bender scene. The day was done, so they both headed home.

After making a pit stop at one of the stores near the Laundromat, Jo drove the police car to her small cottage in the woods. They often took the cars home if they'd been out late. Her own car, a Volkswagen, sat in the lot in town. She liked the Crown Vic better.

She took a cardboard box carefully out of the trunk. On the porch, she balanced the box on her hip and dipped her index finger into the planter full of purple pansies that sat on the porch railing. It was still cold for annuals, but pansies liked the cold. The dirt inside the box was cool and damp.

The wooden screen door of the cottage was thick with layers of chipped paint and squeaked when she pulled it open. The front door had almost as much paint, but the lock was new and shiny, and she put her key in and pushed the door open.

Inside, the cottage was small but cheery. Once a seasonal camp, it had been converted to year-round and had been painted in light colors. Jo had furnished it with comfortable overstuffed furniture from thrift stores and yard sales. It was all chipped, worn paint, large floral and striped prints, and muted colors. She supposed the decorating magazines would have referred to it as cottage chic, but she'd just cobbled together the best value for her budget.

She passed through the living room, the wide pine floorboards creaking as she made her way to the kitchen, which had been remodeled extensively. The ceiling rose up in a peak, and the old wooden cabinets had been painted a sunny shade of yellow. They stretched all the way to the ceiling—too high for Jo to store anything on the top shelf without getting on a step stool even though she was five foot seven.

Jo put the box on the butcher-block countertop. She carefully pulled out the small round goldfish bowl and set it on the counter. She leaned over so her face was at counter height and peered in at the fish. Its orange-gold fins flapped as it turned to face her. She wondered what she looked like from his perspective. Probably just a gigantic distorted face like when you looked in a fun-house mirror.

She took the jar of flake food out of the box and pinched one tiny flake between her index finger and thumb. She dropped it on the surface of the water. The fish zoomed up and devoured it, practically jumping out of the bowl to do so. He must have been hungry.

She contemplated putting another flake in, but Irving down at the pet store had warned her about overfeeding the fish. Too much food produced too much waste and could turn the water toxic. He'd also suggested a small tank with a filter. Fish bowls apparently weren't the best environment for keeping fish in. She'd consider that later—best to see how this worked out first.

She sat at the old farmer's table to admire her new companion. She thought about Lucy with her bright eyes and wagging tail. Reese had taken her back to the shelter. Jo hoped the dog would find a loving family.

Maybe someday she could graduate from a goldfish to something with four legs.

When she'd come to White Rock four years ago, she hadn't expected to be there very long. It had seemed smarter to rent. That way she could pick up and leave once she'd finished her business. She'd told Sam in the interview that she needed a change of pace—someplace more rural. That was only half true. He didn't need to know the real reason she was here. But as time had marched on, she'd come to love the job and love working with Sam. The *real* reason had faded into the background.

She'd never imagined she'd want to put down roots, but she'd come to love her cottage. It was small, but perfect for just one person. Her favorite part was the setting. It was secluded, set by itself in the woods, surrounded by pine trees and wildlife. To the east she had a view of the mountains, and there was a bubbling creek out back. It had the comfortable, secure feeling of home.

She supposed it wouldn't be so bad to settle down here. Maybe she could buy the cottage. She didn't have family to draw her to any other area.

Thoughts of her family stirred unpleasant memories. Images of the empty chair at the table where her eight-year-old sister, Tammy, should have been sitting. Her mother's vacant eyes. Her father's anger. The hollow, empty feeling that Jo should not have had to experience at the tender age of ten.

After Tammy had disappeared, there had been a flurry of activity. People searching. Cops asking questions. Jo had been terrified and intrigued at the same time. And sad. Especially when she would peek into her sister's room every morning, hoping that she'd see Tammy there. Hoping it had all been a bad dream. But instead she saw Tammy's toys sitting alone exactly in the same place Tammy had left them the last afternoon she'd played with them. It was almost a year before her mother even went in the room and picked them up.

Jo had snuck in herself a few times, though. Somehow, she knew her mother wouldn't want her in there. But she'd had to go in. To touch Tammy's favorite purple shirt. To smell the scent of her that still clung to her pillow. To wish her back.

But Tammy never came back.

Eventually, the activity died down. And then Jo was left with only her mother, her father, and her older sister, Bridgett. The idyllic childhood Jo had known up to that point vanished, replaced by a cold and empty existence.

The grief had sent her mother to an early grave and turned her father into a stranger. She hadn't seen him in over a decade. Bridgett had eventually turned to drugs. She lived a few towns over. That was one of the reasons Jo had moved here. But Bridgett had refused all the attempts Jo had made to help her.

She hadn't made a lot of friends since she'd come to town, but that was just as well. Friends would want to come over to her place, and coming over to her place might mean looking through her things, and, well... she couldn't have that.

Sam was about the closest thing to a friend that she had, unless you counted Marisol, who did her hair down at the salon. Sometimes they went out for beers and had even gone shopping a few times together. She liked Mari's quirky sense of humor and her down-home common sense.

But she didn't share nearly as much with Mari as she did with Sam. It made sense because Jo and Sam worked together every day. They had to trust each other; their lives depended on it. But, even so, their relationship had boundaries. Jo and Sam did their hanging out at Spirits. They'd only been to each other's houses a few times. Which was just fine with Jo. She didn't get close to people. What was the point of getting close to someone when they could just be ripped out of your life forever without even a moment's warning?

Jo reached over to the hutch that sat against the wall and pulled out a pencil and pad of paper and started scribbling down clues. Sometimes just brainstorming was a good way to get the mind working on solving a case. But it wasn't just the Palmer case she needed to think about. She hadn't told Sam about seeing Dupont and Thorne going to Lago. She hadn't told him about Kevin lying about being in there either. Truth was, she didn't know if Kevin actually was lying. He only said he didn't have lunch—maybe he was in Lago for some other reason.

It was possible Dupont and Thorne were just there at the same time as a coincidence. It didn't mean they were having some sort of nefarious meeting. Jo knew she shouldn't make assumptions. She'd gotten in trouble for that before at other jobs, but what had happened to her sister had given her a suspicious nature, causing her to always think the worst. Heck, she even suspected there was more to Tyler's shooting than met the eye when she had no good reason to think it.

She didn't want Sam to think she was the type that always jumped to the worst conclusions. She wanted him to value her opinion, and the only way to do that was to back her suspicions up with evidence.

As she scribbled on the pad, she listed out the names of the people who were involved with Lynn, then drew lines radiating out from each one and listed out her various suspicions.

Noah was right in the center. He'd been involved intimately with Lynn. They'd started the company together, and she'd even left her controlling shares to him in her will. Yet he'd neglected to mention that each time they'd asked about motive. The way Jo saw it, that gave him two motives to kill her. One if he was still carrying a torch for her and jealous of her fooling around with other guys, the other to get control of the company.

Oddly enough, she had a sneaking suspicion that Amber was also lying about something. But why? Amber was very possessive when it came to Noah. Maybe she was jealous of the previous relationship. What if Amber wanted to get rid of Lynn to make sure Noah didn't get back together with her?

And where was Lynn's phone?

Jo doodled on the pad. She thought about Dupont and his incessant threats. She thought about Kevin and his trip to Lago. She thought about the dog, Lucy, and she thought about Tyler's shooting. When her thoughts turned around to the suspects on the paper again, she realized that finding Lynn Palmer's killer might be the least of her worries.

CHAPTER SIXTEEN

S am liked his office at the police station because the solid oak door shut out all the noise. He could think better when it was quiet. Even though the office wasn't fancy, it had everything he needed. His doublewide mission oak partners' desk was big enough for laying out all his files. His chair was old but leaned back easily. He even liked the familiar squeak it made when he shifted position.

But his favorite part was the windows. They were ten feet tall and rounded at the tops. Facing north, they framed a majestic view of the mountains. Looking out of these windows, he could watch over the town. He could see the pedestrians going about their business. In summer, it was crowded with the tourists in colorful tee shirts and shorts that flocked to the area for fishing, hiking, and kayaking. In winter, they came for snowmobiling, skiing, and snowshoeing, adorned in ski suits and wool hats.

Right now, though, he didn't have much time for window gazing. He'd gone to visit Lynn Palmer's parents first thing. Talking to parents of a murder victim was always draining, and this morning had been no exception. At least he felt that he'd left them with a little bit of comfort, assuring them that he would seek justice for Lynn.

He hadn't gotten any new information from them other than the name of her lawyer, which they already knew, but he felt better that he could say he'd gotten the name from them. They'd also told him who her cell phone carrier was. Since her phone was still missing, Sam would have to get a court order for whatever records they had on their server. Of course, that could take forever, so it was better if they could find the phone and get the information from it.

On the way back to the office, he'd had to make a side trip. Bullwinkle, the town moose, had caused a ruckus down by Paugus River, which had in turn caused a fender bender when a startled tourist had been watching Bullwinkle and not the road.

Sam had spent a good part of the early morning there sorting things out. Bullwinkle was famous around town, with many of the locals claiming they could recognize him by the shape of his antlers. He even had his own Facebook page where people posted pictures of him when he was sighted around town.

Sam didn't think it was actually the same moose, but he played along. In his mind, frequent sightings meant the moose population was healthy, and that was a good thing. Too much of the local wildlife was dwindling in size because of people like Thorne who were decimating the woods that animals lived in and turning them into hotels and golf courses.

Jo and Kevin had been busy that morning, too, with the usual neighbor squabbles, lost pets, and an old man with Alzheimer's who wandered away from home. Thankfully, someone had discovered him walking down Main Street in his pajamas and taken him into the diner for breakfast while waiting for Jo to pick him up and deliver him safely to his family.

Sam didn't like that the routine calls had delayed his investigation of the murder, but what could he do? Someone had to keep up the police work in the town. If they weren't so shorthanded, he would've had another officer to send out.

He'd had Reese call Noah and Amber in to give their statements after lunch. He wanted to talk to Noah first, seeing as he was the one with the biggest reason to want Lynn dead.

He figured Amber for the weak link. She was closest

to Noah and might know more than she was letting on. Depending on what he learned from them, he'd decide on who to talk to next and what questions to ask. Maybe he'd get lucky and one of them would confess. Either way, the theory of it being Jesse wasn't going to hold water.

On the desk in front of him was a crumpled receipt from the gas station. Jesse had paid with a credit card, the time clearly stamped 2:23 a.m. By Sam's estimation, the campground was ten minutes from the gas station. There was no way Jesse could have killed Lynn between 2:15 and 2:45 if he was at the gas station at 2:23. The killer had shoved her body into the river, and that must've taken some time.

Since they'd been out on calls all morning, Reese had rounded up sandwiches at the deli, and Sam was just finishing up his ham and Swiss. Reese had ordered it with spicy mustard just the way he liked it.

A soft tap sounded at the door.

"Come in."

Kevin poked his head in. "Reese said you wanted to see me?"

Sam gestured at the chair and Kevin came in and shut the door.

"You know we're shorthanded." Why did Sam feel like he was being a traitor to Tyler? He was going to have to hire someone sometime. He was pretty sure Tyler would've understood.

Kevin nodded.

"So I was wondering if you wanted to come on full time. We'd be happy to have you."

Kevin was silent for a minute. He wasn't exactly jumping at the opportunity. The relief that washed over Sam made him realize he didn't really want Kevin to move up to full time. But who would turn down a full-time gig?

"Thanks. I appreciate your confidence in me." Kevin leaned forward in his chair and looked down at his feet, scrubbing his chin. "But the truth is I'm not really looking to go full time."

Sam frowned. "Oh. Okay. Well, I just wanted to offer it to you first."

"It's appreciated. I mean, I can do extra hours and filling in in the interim."

"Okay. Good."

There was an awkward silence, and then Kevin said, "Are we done?"

"Yeah. Oh. Maybe you can head out to the campsite. We can't find the victim's cell phone, and I'm thinking it might've been dropped near where her clothes were found or on the beach. I poked around a little bit there yesterday but didn't do a thorough search. Maybe you could look more closely."

Kevin was halfway to the door. He shot over his shoulder, "Will do."

As he opened the door, Jo was standing outside.

They did an awkward little shuffle in the doorway, and then she poked her head in and said, "You ready, chief? Noah Brickey is here for his statement."

CHAPTER SEVENTEEN

Noah Brickey sat ramrod straight in the uncomfortable wooden chair. They put their suspects in that chair on purpose because one leg was shorter than the rest and it wobbled slightly, keeping the suspect off-balance.

Sam was behind his desk, leaning casually back in his chair, hands clasped loosely in front of him. Jo was in another chair, angled so that she could watch Noah. She had a notepad in her lap on which she was tapping the eraser end of her pencil at an annoying rate. Tap. Tap. Tap. Like water torture.

She thought she saw a bead of sweat on Noah's brow despite the fact that it was cool inside the police station.

"I have in my notes that you and Miss Palmer started Lyah software together," Sam said.

"We started it in college. The name, Lyah, is a play on the letters in our first names."

"Clever," Sam said.

"And you were lovers?" Jo added.

Noah swiveled his gaze to Jo, his brow creasing. "We were, but that was a long time ago. We broke up."

"Was this breakup amicable, or was there a lot of fighting?" Sam asked.

Noah swiveled his head back toward Sam, appearing to become slightly agitated. "There were a few fights, but then we ended up being friends. I mean, we have to work together, so we have to get along. We're good friends now."

"Uh-huh. And you're with Amber now," Sam said.

Noah looked momentarily confused, then his expression cleared. "Yes, Amber Huffman. She's a receptionist at work. We've been dating for a couple of months now."

"Really? That's not awkward?" Jo asked, causing Noah to swivel his head back to her again. "I mean, your ex-girlfriend and your current girlfriend working together and hanging out together? Seems like that could be opportunity for a lot of fighting."

Noah became belligerent, his voice rising. "What does this have to do with Lynn's death? Surely you don't think I killed her because I'm dating another woman. What about that local guy? He seemed like a lowlife. You should have him in here."

"Couldn't have been him." Sam pushed the gas station receipt on his desk toward Noah. "He was pumping gas at the time of death."

Noah looked down at the receipt then up at Sam. "If you're accusing me, I want a lawyer."

"We're not accusing you. We're just trying to figure out the group dynamics and find out what happened that night. You have to admit that jealousy from an ex would be a powerful motive, but you moved on, and she didn't have a boyfriend... unless you were jealous of Lynn paying attention to Jesse," Sam said.

Noah relaxed. "No, I wasn't. It doesn't make sense that I would kill her. If anyone would've killed her because of jealousy, it would be Amber..." His words trailed off, and his face scrunched. "Well, surely you guys don't think it was Amber? I mean, she wouldn't hurt a fly."

Jo thought about how Jesse had said he'd heard Lynn arguing with the blonde. Amber was the only blonde in the group, and it wouldn't be the first time she'd caught a killer who had murdered her boyfriend's ex. Especially if they were as close as Noah and Lynn had once been.

Noah swiveled his head between them, stopping at Jo. "No way. There was nothing for them to fight about. I mean, the whole trip was Lynn's idea, and she encouraged me to bring Amber. Neither one of us still had romantic feelings toward each other, so why would Amber be jealous?"

Sam leaned forward, the creaking of the old chair capturing Noah's attention and causing his head to swivel back in Sam's direction. "How come you didn't tell us that you get all of Lynn's shares in the company now?"

Noah looked momentarily confused, and then, as if a light bulb had switched on, he sucked in a breath. "Of course. I'd forgotten about that. When we started the company, we wanted to make sure it could still be run the way we wanted if anything happened. The lawyer recommended that we give each other controlling shares in our will... But you don't think I would kill her for that? The company isn't even doing that well."

"But you said that you had all just been working long hours to put out a new game. What if that game took off? The company could be worth a lot, couldn't it?" Sam asked.

Noah spread his arms. "Sure, but if it was, I'd have plenty of money. I wouldn't need to kill Lynn for her shares."

Sam nodded slowly. "Can you think of anyone who *would* want her dead?"

"No. That's the thing. Everyone liked her. That's why I figured it was someone we didn't know, like that Jesse guy. Maybe it was someone else, someone from the campground. Like another camper. Some people from another campsite joined us for a while. It could have been one of them, couldn't it?" Noah turned pleading eyes on Jo and then Sam.

"Maybe, but I wouldn't count on it."

CHAPTER EIGHTEEN

S am had been watching the expression on Jo's face while they were interviewing Noah. He could tell that she didn't believe everything he had said, and neither did Sam. They didn't have a chance to compare notes, though, because as soon as Noah left, Amber entered.

Amber perched on the edge of the wooden chair, her knees pressed together, her red-tipped nails clutching the armrests. She looked like a murderer ready to be sentenced.

"I don't think I can tell you very much. I didn't really know Lynn, and I wasn't paying much attention to her that night," she said.

Sam got straight to the point. "We heard you had a fight with her in the bar."

Alarm crossed her pretty features. The chair rocked slightly. "Who said that?"

"We have our sources." Sam leaned across the desk. "Is it true?"

Amber looked at the floor. "No."

Sam figured Amber was lying. He glanced at Jo for confirmation. Jo nodded.

"Are you sure, Amber? Because lying would be obstructing justice, and there's jail time for that."

Her eyes flew up to his face. "Well, maybe we had a little argument, but that doesn't mean I killed her."

Sam leaned back in his chair. "Of course not. Why don't you tell me all about it."

Amber sighed. "You probably already know that Lynn used to date Noah. They started the company together. And I think she still wanted to get her hooks into him. When we were in the bar, she was flirting with that long-haired guy and with Noah, too. Well, I don't like anyone getting their claws into my man, so I laid into her." Amber grimaced. "Okay, maybe I had a few too many to drink, but she was out of line."

"That was in the bar—what about later on at the campsite?" Sam asked.

"What about it? We came back. We partied. As far as I know, she was still alive when Noah and I went into our tent."

"Can you specifically say that you saw her alive when you went to bed?" Jo asked.

Amber looked down at the floor. "I think so. I did have a bit much to drink, and things are a little fuzzy. But I remember her with that guy."

"He has an alibi," Sam said.

Her face pinched together. "Oh. Well, I don't know what more I can tell you."

"Do you happen to know where her phone is?" Jo asked.

Amber shook her head. "No. After you came this afternoon, we all looked all around the site, but none of us found it. It's the weirdest thing. I know she had one."

"And besides her flirting with Noah at the bar, did you see them together any other time?"

Amber's eyes narrowed. "What do you mean *together*? They weren't together. I was with him the whole time."

"What time did you go to bed?" Sam asked.

She thought about it. "It must've been around two-thirty, because we left the bar at one, and we weren't up much longer."

"And you went into the tent at the same time as Noah?"

"Yeah. Of course I did."

"And you were both in there the whole time after that?"

Her eyes flicked to the window. She crossed her arms over her chest. "Of course. I was with Noah all night, so he couldn't have killed her, if that's what you're getting at."

"Is there anything else? Any idea who might have done this? Did you notice anything odd maybe the day before when you were in town or that night at the bar?" Sam asked.

Amber narrowed her eyes as she thought. "I don't know if I would say this was necessarily odd, but Lynn acted kind of strange when we were planning the trip."

"How so?"

"We talked about different places to go camping, but she insisted we come here. And the day she died, we all went downtown for groceries. She suggested we split up and do some shopping. You know, check out the local shops and stuff. It was all kind of spur of the moment and casual." Amber leaned forward in the chair, her face animated, as if she was suddenly realizing what she was saying could be important. "But Lynn wasn't acting very casual. She was acting like she had an appointment, and when Julie, Tara and I came out of the secondhand store, Lynn was nowhere to be found."

CHAPTER NINETEEN

A fter Amber left, Sam and Jo took a break and headed for the coffee maker. Jo had finished her cup during the interview with Noah, and her brain was begging for the sharp tang of caffeine. It was also begging for a jelly donut, but there were none in the station.

Sam let her go first. She leaned her shoulder against the wall, her finger tapping on the mug as she watched him pop his orange K-Cup in and slide the dark-blue police-insignia mug underneath. Jo went back over the interviews in her brain while she waited for his cup to fill.

During the interviews, she'd studied both Noah and Amber for the little "tells" that would indicate they were lying. A twitch here, a furtive glance there. They both hadn't been straight about something.

"I don't think either one of them was being straight with us," Jo said.

Sam opened a packet of sugar and poured it into his coffee. "And what was that bit about the meeting? Do you think Lynn really had a meeting, or was Amber lying about that?"

"Why would she make that up?"

"And why did Lynn insist they camp here? Do you think Amber made that up to try to throw off suspicion? To make us think she had a local connection to who killed her?"

"Maybe she *did* have a local connection. This is where her cell phone would help tremendously. I hope Kevin finds it."

"Reese's got the paperwork to subpoena Verizon for her phone records, but that could take a while. At least Dupont won't try to block that."

"The way he's been hounding us, he'll probably rush it through, but what they have on the servers might not include what we need. Not everything is stored. Having the phone would be best."

The door opened, and Kevin came in, heading straight for the coffee maker. "Thank God, coffee."

Jo noticed he was empty handed. "You didn't find her cell phone?"

Kevin pressed his lips together and shook his head. "Afraid not. I looked all over that area and didn't find a thing except dirt, leaves, and rocks."

"Hey, guys, I hate to interrupt, but a bunch of calls came in when you were taking those statements." Reese, who had just come in through the front door, picked up several pink slips of paper off her desk and waved them in the air.

"What have you got?" Sam asked.

She looked at the slips. "Stolen pickles at the general store—Arty's holding the culprit for you. Joan Freemont called to complain about a fight between Nettie Deardorff and Rita Hoelscher." She looked up at them over the slips. "Said it was getting violent. And there's been a disturbance reported over at the Rock Ledge campground."

Jo's brows shot up, and she looked at Sam. "You think that has something to do with our case?"

Sam had already put the mug down and was heading for the door. "I don't know, but I'm going to find out. The other calls are urgent too. Jo, you take the general store, and Kevin, you go see what's up with Rita and Nettie. Everybody radio in when you're done."

KEVIN GOT into his Isuzu and headed out to Prospect Hill, where Joan Freemont lived. He wouldn't mind having to drive his own car all the time if he didn't always get stuck with all the crappy jobs. But that had always been the way.

Jo, Sam, and Tyler had always taken all the good calls, and Kevin had gotten the scraps. He was always the one that had to decorate the big tree in the green at Christmas, risking his life on the rickety ladder and going home full of pine pitch and needles. And he always got stuck with traffic duty on the Fourth of July. Not to mention how they always seemed to saddle him with picking up the drunk and disorderlies, who would puke all over him. At least they let him drive the Crown Vic with the screen between the front and back seats on those calls.

Of course, being the one to get the crappy calls did have a lot to do with him being the only part-timer, and by the time he came on shift, that was mostly what was left. Because the important stuff was usually the most urgent.

Still, it wasn't just the calls. It was the way the three of them had treated him. Like he wasn't a real part of the team. Maybe if they'd treated him like he belonged, then he wouldn't have done what he had earlier that year.

Thoughts of what he had done sent a jolt of anxiety through him. Maybe he shouldn't have been so quick to think that Sam and Jo didn't see him as their equal.

When Sam had offered him the full-time position this morning, he'd been surprised. He'd thought they didn't want him, but now... well, it was too late. He'd already formed his alliances, and now that he had, he didn't need that full-time pay. Maybe Sam and Jo should have started treating him better *before* Tyler died.

Thoughts of Tyler's death brought on another jolt of anxiety. He sure hoped the few bits of information he'd passed along didn't have anything to do with what happened to Tyler. But if it had, that was because Tyler had been up to something bad. And if Tyler had been breaking the law, then Kevin had done the right thing, hadn't he?

Kevin wanted to believe he had, but doubts swirled in his mind like a flock of vultures. What if he'd acted too hastily? His father had always told him he was too quick to leap before he looked.

It couldn't have been his fault—Tyler had been killed by a crazy auto thief—that had nothing to do with the information Kevin had been asked to look for. And, besides, he hadn't found anything worth passing on. Not even after volunteering to clean out Tyler's desk. No photos. No notes. Nothing.

After that, Kevin had thought his little task for The Big Guy was done, but the other day, he'd been summoned to the meeting place behind Lago, and the note he'd gotten said otherwise. He didn't know if he could keep trying to dig up bits of information without blowing his cover.

Jo had sounded suspicious when she'd asked if he'd lunched at Lago. He'd panicked and said no, and now he realized that had been a big mistake. Her desk window faced that side of the street, and she'd probably seen him. The last thing he wanted was for Sam or Jo to find out what he'd done. He should have told her he was visiting his cousin who worked there. That part was true. He just didn't need to tell her the part about the note with the instructions he'd pocketed during the quick meeting *behind* the restaurant.

As he came to the crest of the hill, he saw Joan Freemont standing in Nettie Deardorff's front yard. She was wearing a pink bathrobe, her arms crossed over her chest. Nettie and Rita Hoelscher were standing on either side of the white picket fence that divided their yards, yelling at each other. Nettie raised her index finger and wagged it in Rita's face. Rita grabbed it and twisted.

The goat—what was its name? Betty or Bessy?—hopped around at Rita's feet, stopping every few seconds to nibble on her long brown skirt.

Kevin parked on the side of the street. He really did hate these calls. So what if Sam had rescued a cat from a tree and Jo had handled the dispute at the Laundromat the other night? The truth was that *he* was the one that got them the most.

If he had accepted the full-time job, would things be different? They'd hire another part-timer, and maybe the new guy would get all the crappy calls. But then Kevin would be working full time with Sam and Jo, and he wasn't sure he'd fit in. He just didn't click with them.

He didn't need the money, anyway. He patted the note that was still in his pocket. Not now that he had this little side job. The side job was easy. All he had to do was keep his eyes and ears open and report back specific pieces of information. It paid more than a full-time police salary, and he was still helping to serve justice in some way. Or at least that was what he told himself.

He got out of the car and headed toward the old ladies, the note crinkling ominously in his pocket as he crossed the street.

CHAPTER TWENTY

S am would have preferred to talk to the rest of the campers right after Noah and Amber, but the three disturbance calls that had come in were of an urgent nature and took precedence.

Then again, letting Amber and Noah report back to the others so they could all stew about it overnight could work in their favor. Might make the killer nervous. And nervous killers were bound to screw up.

Too bad the interviews had only left Sam with more questions. Maybe this disturbance at the campground would answer some of those questions.

He careened into the main parking lot, sirens blaring and lights flashing. Ellie ran out to meet him.

"There's a dog running loose down by the river, barking and making all kinds of ruckus. It's scaring the kids, and the campers are complaining."

Sam's stomach sank. Lucy? Hopefully she hadn't found another body in the river.

He headed toward the river. Sure enough, Lucy was there at the bank, barking and pacing. When she saw him, she stopped and ran over to him.

Sam crouched down to her level and patted her neck, his eyes scanning the water. No body. "I guess you ran away again? Don't like the accommodations at the pound?"

"*Woof!*"

Lucy swung around and splashed back into the water then looked back at Sam as if wanting him to follow.

"You want to swim? You're gonna ruin all that nice work they did on your fur."

Lucy did a half spin then planted her feet in front of her, those whiskey eyes demanding his attention. She barked again, this time low and insistent. She stuck her nose in the water then jerked it out, flinging drops around. She looked back at Sam as if she were hoping he wasn't too stupid to get the message.

Sam splashed out to her. This was the rocky part of the river, and the water was only about five inches deep. At least this time he didn't have his dress shoes on; his solid black boots were already in pretty bad shape.

The river was crystal clear. You could see every rock and grain of sand. In the slower-running sections, you could see tiny baby fish when the sunlight slanted in at just the right angle.

Lucy had her eyes fixed on a large gray rock. It was flat on the top, and something dark that wasn't a rock or sand or anything natural looked to be wedged underneath it.

Sam reached into the freezing-cold water, pried the rock up, grabbed the thing underneath it, and pulled it out.

It was a cell phone.

SAM HANDLED the cell phone gingerly, trying not to touch too much of it even though he knew the water had already washed off any fingerprints or DNA evidence. He wasn't even sure it was Lynn's or that anything could be recovered from it.

He rummaged an evidence bag out of the crime scene kit in the back of the Tahoe and slipped the phone into it. Lucy sat at his heels, looking up as if awaiting his praise.

"Yes, you did a good job. Seems like you've got quite a nose for police work."

Lucy gazed up at him. She looked happy. Her face almost looked as if she were smiling. Her thick, furry tail swished back and forth excitedly.

"But I can't keep you."

Lucy still looked happy, but her tail swishing slowed down.

"If you're hungry, maybe I could get you a burger."

Her tail swishing sped up again.

Sam hated the idea of taking the dog back to the shelter. What did they even feed them in there? Probably some kind of generic kibble. The least he could do was get her a burger at Spirits. Maybe one of the specialty burgers.

Sam wondered what kinds of add-ons dogs liked. Hadn't he heard that some "people" food was toxic for them? Better to get her a plain burger or maybe that pot roast from the diner that she liked.

Sam opened the tailgate. "Okay, get in."

Lucy hopped in and immediately trotted up front to the passenger seat, leaving a trail of wet, sandy footprints along the way.

Sam just shook his head and smiled. The fur on Lucy's legs and belly was soaked from being in the river, and the passenger seat would be all wet. That was Jo's problem, though. She was the only one that ever sat there.

He was just pulling out of the campground when the police radio in the car crackled. It was Reese. "Sam, I just got a call in. There is a disturbance down at Holy Spirits. Fight in progress, and it looks like a bad one."

Sam flipped on the siren and stepped on the gas.

THE INSIDE of Holy Spirits looked as if a tornado had ripped through it. It smelled of beer, sweat, and anger. The air buzzed with excitement.

One table was overturned, three chairs lay on their sides, and the bar patrons were standing in a circle. Two large men stood in the middle. Judging by the swollen lip on one and the shiner already making an appearance on the other, Sam knew they'd already been fighting for a while.

"Break it up! White Rock Police!" Sam pushed his way through the crowd, holding out his badge. There was no need for the badge—everyone in the bar knew him. Especially the two men fighting.

Jerry Vetter and Ed Clough hated each other. It was all because of Lily Simmons. She'd been dating Ed when Jerry caught her eye five years ago when they were seniors in high school. Lily and Jerry were married now.

You'd think Ed would've gotten over it by now, but occasionally, he started it up with Jerry all over again. Typically in the bar after a few beers. It usually only amounted to a few black eyes and sometimes broken fingers. But Sam had to stop the fight just the same.

"He's got this coming, Chief." Ed addressed Sam but kept his eyes on Jerry.

"Come on, Ed. You know fighting never solves

anything. All it does is get you with some doctor bills."
Sam's tone was casual, but his body was tense, waiting
to take action if the fighting got bad. Sometimes he let
them throw a few punches and get it out of their
system. If things got too rough, he'd have to jump in.

"Bastard ruined my life." Ed swung again, his fist
connecting with Jerry's chin.

Jerry's face jerked to the right. Spittle and flecks of
blood flew outward. The crowd jumped back.

Jerry turned toward Ed, anger gleaming in his eyes.
He punched Ed first in the stomach, then the chin. Ed
staggered back then whirled around, picking up one of
the chairs and holding it over his head.

Sam jumped in between them, holding his hand
out. "You don't want to do that, Ed. Willful destruction
of property. Billie might sue you."

Ed swung the chair anyway. Sam barreled into him,
disrupting the force of the blow. The chair grazed painfully
off his shoulder and smashed to the floor, one leg cracking
loudly as it splintered off from the bottom of the seat.

Ed turned his anger on Sam. "What'd you do that
for? I need to finish this guy off once and for all."

"This isn't the way to settle things." Sam put his
hand gently on Ed's arm in an attempt to calm him.

Ed pulled back his fist. Apparently, he'd forgotten
that his beef was with Jerry and was going to continue
to lash out at anyone in front of him. Even Sam.

"Don't do it, Ed. Assaulting an officer of the law isn't something you want to get into."

The words made Ed hesitate for a second, then he crouched down and rushed Sam, barreling shoulder first into his stomach and knocking him to the floor. Before Sam knew what had happened, the two of them were rolling around on the floor, fists flying.

Sam was a good fighter, but Ed must've been taking lessons. He got Sam into a stranglehold, increasing the force on his windpipe. Sam smelled stale beer and cigar smoke on his hot breath.

"Hey, Ed, cut that out. That's the chief." This was Jerry's voice, ironically.

Sam kicked back, connecting with Ed's shin. Ed loosened his grip slightly, just enough to allow Sam to break free.

Sam spun around in time to see Ed stagger back a few steps. Then Ed pulled a fist. Sam got ready to dodge. He didn't want to hit Ed if he didn't have to. Even though he was within his right to break up a fight, it was better if you didn't have to leave a mark on someone. You never knew when the public would believe a claim of police brutality. He just hoped Ed would tire out before Sam had to hurt him in order to get him to stop.

Sam didn't have to worry about that for long. A hulking figure stepped in between them, brought up his fist, and popped Ed right in the face, sending him crumbling to the floor.

Mick Gervasi turned to face Sam, a grin spreading on his face. "You gotta work on your street-fighting skills, Chief. I can't always be around to get you out of trouble."

CHAPTER TWENTY-ONE

"I could've taken care of Ed myself," Sam said as he peeled the buns off the burger he'd ordered at the bar. He squinted at the bare patty. Ketchup and mayonnaise were smeared all over the surface. He looked over at Mick. "Are ketchup and mayo bad for dogs?"

Mick shrugged.

Lucy whined, and Sam looked down at her. "You like ketchup?"

He scraped it off anyway. It didn't seem like something a dog should be eating. Then he threw the burger into a bowl and set it on the floor. Lucy sniffed it cautiously.

"Beggars can't be choosers there, buddy." Sam pressed his fingers against his bottom lip. It was sore where one of the punches had cut the inside of his mouth. He could still taste the coppery tang of his blood.

Mick leaned back in the kitchen chair. He was still wearing his leather jacket, and the deep pockets bulged out, the right one more so than the left. The amber-colored beer bottle in his hand tilted slightly as he leaned.

"I figured you could've taken care of him, but it looked like that might have taken a while. I didn't want to wait around. Got important information." His gaze flicked from Sam to the dog. "When did you get a dog?"

Sam joined him at the table with his own beer. He glanced at Lucy, who was licking the sides of the bowl. "She's a stray."

"You keeping her?"

Sam's heart pinched. "Nah. Got no time. I had picked her up on another call and happened to have her in the truck when I was called to the fight. Figured the shelter would be closed by the time we were done, so I brought her here."

"Maybe you should let her stay. She'd be a lot better female companionship than either one of your ex-wives."

Sam laughed. Mick's words had a ring of truth. Because Sam and Mick had been friends since they were young boys, Mick had known both of Sam's wives well. He hadn't approved of either of them. Maybe Sam should have listened to him.

"Jo would be good female companionship too," Mick continued.

"Jo and I work together. She's off-limits."

Sam hadn't really considered Jo as female companionship in that way. He liked her and respected her. He couldn't imagine not having her in his life every day. But as a fellow officer. Not a girlfriend. She was attractive enough, but Sam didn't have a place in his life for a woman, and especially not one where the relationship was going to screw up the workings of his whole police department.

Mick just sipped his beer and shrugged.

Sam's eyes narrowed. Maybe Mick wasn't speaking about Jo being company for Sam.

"She's off limits to you, too." With Mick's black hair, steely blue eyes, and linebacker build, he never had trouble getting women, even now when he was pushing forty. The way Mick ran through women, he didn't want to subject Jo to him.

"Ed sure was mad," Mick said, changing the subject.

"Yep. Always the same thing."

"That's what women will do to you."

"Can't argue with that." Sam swigged his beer. "Good thing he didn't press charges against you."

Mick smirked. "Right. Good thing he came to his senses and realized pressing charges against me might result in you pressing charges against him. Apparently, assaulting a police officer wasn't something he wanted on his record."

Lucy finished licking the bowl and lay down next to Sam's chair.

Mick got up and paced around the kitchen. It wasn't a big room, so the pacing didn't last long.

He stopped at the low wall divider that separated the kitchen from the living room. Gram had made Gramps widen the doorway and put that in when Sam was in his teens. The top of the divider was table-height, and it had bookshelves underneath on either side. Gram had used the surface as a buffet area to spread the desserts out on during holidays.

Mick picked up a birchwood-framed photograph of Sam's girls that was sitting on top. It was Sam's favorite picture, both girls in bright ski jackets with a snowy mountain behind them. Mick's lips quirked in a smile as he looked at it. He had a special place in his heart for Hayley and Marla, and the girls felt the same way about their "Uncle" Mick. Mick had never married or had kids. Sam figured the girls were like a surrogate family.

"You heard from them?" Mick asked.

"Yep. Hayley just got done with finals. And Marla is finishing up her internship. They're planning a visit soon." Thoughts of the impending visit brought on a pang of emptiness. He missed his daughters, but they were grown women now with their own lives in towns far away. He couldn't expect them to hang around here.

"I can't wait to see them." Mick put the picture down and leaned his hip against the bookcase. Sam was glad Gram had made Gramps secure it to the floor.

"So, what were you in such a hurry to see me about?" Sam asked.

"I got something for you." Mick tossed his beer into the trash next to Sam, opened the fridge, and pulled out another one.

Sam leaned over and retrieved the bottle from the trash and threw it in the blue recycling bin by the door. The glass clanked against the other bottles. Mick twisted off the top of his beer, flicked it into the bin, and came back to sit at the table.

"I did some research on that lady who had the car stolen. Barbara Bartles. Turns out she has a grandson that isn't exactly an upstanding citizen." Mick took a slow sip of the beer. "Got to thinking that maybe the car theft wasn't so random."

"He into drugs?" Sam thought about the trace of cocaine and partial fingerprint in the ashtray.

"Yep. Nothing on his record, but I have an in with the police down there, and he's been taken in on suspicion a few times. They went easy on him, hoping he'll eventually inform on the next guy up the chain."

Sam nodded. It was the same thing Sam was hoping

to do with Jesse. "Think it has anything to do with Thorne?"

Mick shrugged. "He lives in Preston, but we don't know how far Thorne's influence reaches. Or even if Thorne is the source of these drugs."

Sam knew he was. Even though they didn't have any proof, it wasn't just wishful thinking. Thorne was up to more than just raping the land to build his resort. But this wasn't about Thorne—this was about Tyler and catching the guy who had killed him.

Sam felt a spark of excitement. This kid could know something about what happened that night. Possibly even be Tyler's killer himself. "What's this kid's name? Maybe we should go talk to him. You know, off the record. See if he knows anything."

Mick reached into his pocket, the grin spreading across his face. He pulled out a plastic bag with a shot glass in it. Sam had been wondering when he was going to show him what he had in there.

"I can do you one better," Mick said. "You know how you got that partial print from the car? I happen to have had a few drinks with Danny Bartles. He drinks shots of Sambuca. And it just so happens that I know the bartender at the bar he hangs out at. She's a pretty blond thing. Anyway, I persuaded her to give me the glass Danny drank from. Might be a print on there you could use."

CHAPTER TWENTY-TWO

Since everyone had touched base as instructed on the previous night's calls, no one was surprised when Sam showed up with Lucy and the remains of Lynn's cell phone the next morning.

Reese found a charger that fit the phone, and now it was sitting on Kevin's desk, and they were all standing around the desk, looking down at it. The screen was loaded with spiderweb cracks, and the back of the case had two chunks of plastic missing. It should have been fully charged, but wouldn't turn on. No surprise, given the shape of the device.

"So the killer probably tossed the phone in after Lynn," Jo said.

"Must have figured something on there might implicate them. Probably hoped it would never be found," Sam added.

"But the killer didn't know we had our secret weapon, right, girl?" Reese leaned down and rubbed Lucy's head. The dog thumped her tail on the floor and glanced from Sam to Reese. Sam swore the darn thing was smiling.

Sam scrubbed his fingers through his short hair. "Too bad we can't get anything off it. It's going to take forever to get the information from Verizon, and meanwhile, the killer has time to cover his tracks."

"Can I try?" Reese reached a tentative hand toward the phone.

"You think you can get it to work?" Sam was dubious. Then again, Reese did have a talent for computers. What the heck? The thing was dead as a doornail—it certainly couldn't hurt to have her try.

"Maybe. If not, I might be able take it to the academy and get someone to work on it." She looked up at Sam hopefully. "It could be quicker than waiting on the carrier to hand over the records."

"Okay, sure."

Reese smiled then cocked her head. "Did something happen to your lip?"

"Nope." Sam knew they'd all heard he went to break up the fight. They didn't need to know the details.

Reese shrugged then took the phone to her desk. Lucy trotted along behind her.

Kevin's eyes followed the dog. "What happens if Dupont comes in and sees the dog here?"

Sam got the impression Kevin wasn't exactly a dog lover. He skirted around Lucy as if she would bite. From the sideways glances Lucy gave Kevin, the feeling was mutual. And it was obvious Kevin didn't want to get on Dupont's bad side, which was somewhat of a mystery considering he didn't seem to care too much about his job.

"Maybe we should keep her in my office. That way if Dupont comes in, I'll come out to talk to him and leave her in there. He won't know she's here," Sam said.

"We can't just hide her in the police station," Kevin said.

"It's just temporary. She has to go back to the shelter. But she helped find the phone, and I'd like to reward her with some free time before she has to go sit in a lonely kennel over there."

"How is she going to get adopted if she's not over there?" Kevin asked.

Sam looked at Lucy, her eyes reflecting all the trust in the world. He wasn't keen on the idea of *someone else* adopting her, but he knew it was the best thing for her.

"She might not get adopted," Reese said in a low voice.

Jo's brow furrowed. "Why not?"

"She's a runner. She's already run away twice. Not too many people want to adopt a dog like that."

"What do you mean? What will they do with her, then?" Sam asked.

Reese glanced at Lucy, who was now lying beside her desk, and lowered her voice. "Eric said they might swap her with another shelter, but if nobody adopts her after a while, she could be euthanized."

As if she knew what they were talking about, Lucy whined. She put her chin on her front paws. Her eyes looked up, her brows twitching as she switched her attention from Reese to Sam to Jo.

"We can't let that happen. She's already helped us out twice. She's practically an officer." Jo looked at Sam. Her gray eyes sparked with alarm.

Sam rubbed his hand over his chin, rough with stubble even at this early time in the morning. Had he forgotten to shave? The glass Mick had given him was burning a hole in the pocket of his windbreaker. He couldn't wait to tell Jo about it. "I don't know what we can do. I wish we could work something out, but..."

"There might be something..." Reese chewed her bottom lip. "Maybe for now we could just try to keep her with us for a little while. I'll see if Eric can reset her time at the shelter so she has more time to get adopted before they trade her out."

"And if she doesn't?" Jo asked.

"Let's just buy her a few days," Reese said. "The shelter only gives them so many days, but if we can make it look like she's a new surrender, then she'll have that much more of a chance. If that doesn't work, I might have something else I can try."

"Okay." Jo looked dubious. "I guess that's all we can do."

Sam nodded. "Fine by me. In the meantime, let's just make sure Dupont doesn't find out we have her."

CHAPTER TWENTY-THREE

I t was a light crime day, and no calls had come in. Sam assigned Kevin to any new disruptions so that he and Jo could focus on interviewing the rest of the campers. He owed it to the Palmers to solve this as quickly as he could.

Sam gave Reese orders to call the other campers in. Hopefully, with Kevin on the call-outs, he and Jo would have enough time to get through the rest of the interviews that afternoon.

He retired to his office with Lucy and called Jo in after him. Kevin looked a little put out that he wasn't in on the interviews, but Jo was a sergeant. Kevin was an officer—a lower rank. With no official detectives on the force, it made sense that Sam and Jo would take on the detective work. If Kevin wanted the better work, he'd have to earn it. Turning down the full-time job wouldn't help.

Jo sat in the chair. "I really hope Reese can find something on that phone, but I'm not optimistic. What do you think we—"

Her words were cut off when Sam put the glass on his desk.

"What's that?"

"Mick gave it to me last night. There's a print on it. Could lead to Tyler's killer."

"What? How did he get it?"

Sam relayed what Mick had told her while he dug the fingerprint dusting kit out of the bottom drawer of his desk. He slipped the glass out of the bag and dusted. There were several prints on it, and he lifted them all.

"So what do you figure? We test it against the partial print we found in the car?" Jo asked.

"Yep."

"And if it is the same guy, what then?"

"Punish him to the fullest extent of the law."

"The prints won't hold up. What about chain of custody? Mick got the fingerprints illegally." Jo tapped the eraser end of her pencil on the pad of paper. "We have to figure out another way. We can't test these prints officially because there'll be a record of it. And if this comes to trial, then even the greenest lawyer will use that against us."

"Yeah, I figured that. We need to know if this guy is involved first, *then* we can figure out the legal way to get him for it. 'Course, we could just go down and beat everything he knows out of him right now. But I figure it's better to see if the print matches—that way we know we're barking up the right tree. If we go down there and we don't have something solid to threaten him with, it gives him time to cover his bases, and we lose the advantage."

"Putting the match through the computer could screw things up for us later." Jo thought for a while. "We need a way to match up the print that isn't recorded officially. And who do we know that has access to crime labs at an academic level that isn't recorded officially?"

"Reese? But we can't ask her to do this. Can we?"

Lucy's tail thumped against Sam's chair as if she were giving her opinion that this was a great idea.

"Of course we can. She cared about Tyler just as much as we did. She wants to see his killer put away too," Jo said.

"I don't know." Sam glanced at the door. "We don't want to let too many people in on the fact that we're not doing things strictly by the book."

"Speaking of that, is Kevin coming on board full time?" Jo asked.

"No."

They stared at each other for a few beats. Nothing

needed to be said. They were both relieved that Kevin wasn't going to be full time.

"I guess we'll have to get used to a new person, then. All the more reason to have Reese on our side." Jo pushed up from the chair and paced over to the long windows. She looked out at the mountains. "We're not doing anything that bad. We're just trying to expedite things. Stuff moves so slowly up here. And it won't be so bad to have Reese on our team—she could get a lot done for us."

"She does seem to have mad computer skills and resources..."

There was a soft tap on the door, and Reese poked her head in. "I figured I'd let you know. The campers are on their way. Should be here in a few minutes."

Sam motioned for Reese to enter and then gestured for her to close the door. She was a quick study, her eyes darkening with understanding as they flicked from the glass, now with black dust on it, to Sam and Jo.

"Reese," Sam started. "I think you know sometimes we might have to push the envelope a little for the sake of justice."

Reese's eyes lit up. "Oh, I totally understand. Like with the phone."

Sam smiled, his eyes meeting Jo's. "Exactly like with the phone. And if you're on board with that, I have a way you might be instrumental in finding Tyler's killer."

CHAPTER TWENTY-FOUR

Jo and Sam figured the best person to talk to next in the Palmer case was Julie. Jo had noticed she seemed a little hesitant when they'd been at the campsite. She was hiding something, and Jo wanted to find out what it was.

Reese ushered Julie into the room. She was dressed in camping attire—camouflage pants, tee shirt, light-blue windbreaker, hiking boots, and a wide-brimmed ball cap. She sat nervously in the chair on the other side of Sam's desk. Sam made her wait, pretending he was looking through paperwork. Jo could feel the tension in the room as Julie shifted around in her seat, causing the chair to rock and jolt on its uneven legs.

"Sorry, Miss Swan. I was just looking through my notes here from when I talked to Amber and Noah."

Sam leaned back in his chair and steepled his fingers. "So how long had you known Lynn?"

Julie's eyes misted, and she sniffed. "Four years. We were all friends. Lynn and Noah started the company. They asked me to work for them. I was third on board."

"So you knew Lynn pretty well, then?" Jo asked.

"You could say that. We all hung around together a lot. We worked long hours, so we became kind of like an extended family."

"And how would you say Lynn felt about Noah taking up with Amber?" Sam asked.

Julie's brows drew together. "Lynn didn't care. She was the one that broke up with Noah."

"And what about Amber? Was she jealous of their former relationship?" Jo asked. When they had interrogated Amber, Jo had gotten the impression Amber was lying about both her and Noah being in the tent. Jo wasn't sure if Amber was the killer. She didn't know if there was a big enough motive there, but she wasn't being truthful about something. Maybe digging into what Julie knew would uncover what that something was.

Julie snorted. "I'll say. You ask me, she was just a rebound girl for Noah. She doesn't have a lot of self-confidence, always clutching at him and crowding him. I don't expect that to last long. But... well... that has nothing to do with what happened to Lynn, right?" Julie looked as if she might've wanted to say more but held

TELLING LIES

off. Maybe the realization that Sam and Jo were doing a little bit more than just taking a statement had her nervous that she'd said too much already.

"So you think Noah was going to break things off with Amber?" Sam asked. "Maybe Amber caught wind of that. Maybe Amber thought Noah was going to go back to Lynn. Maybe Amber tried to make sure that wouldn't happen."

Julie gasped. "You don't think Amber would kill Lynn? Over that?"

"Someone killed her. We're trying to figure out the motive. Do you know why anyone would want her dead?"

Julie shook her head. "I told you before. No idea."

"What about the breakup with Noah? How did that affect the company? Is that when the company started failing?"

"No. I don't think that had anything to do with it. We're all professionals. Sure, at first it was kind of awkward, but after a while, that all passed." Julie shrugged. "Anyway, that was almost a year ago."

"And they still wanted to have equal shares in the company? Seems like that might be problematic eventually," Sam said.

"I wouldn't know anything about that," Julie said.

"Maybe one of them was trying to phase the other one out to get control of the company before this new game was released," Jo suggested.

"What are you saying? That Noah killed Lynn to get control of the company? Noah wouldn't do that, and besides, wouldn't her share go to her family or something?"

"Actually, no," Sam said. "When they started the company, they agreed to leave each other controlling shares. Of course, they probably didn't think they would be breaking up when they agreed to that. Maybe Noah wanted to make sure she didn't have a chance to change the agreement."

"Noah wouldn't do something like that!"

Julie seemed adamant, but Jo wasn't so sure.

"Where were you that night around 2:30 a.m.?" Sam asked.

"Now you're accusing me?" Julie straightened in the chair, causing it to tip to the left. "Do I need a lawyer?"

Sam held his palms up. "We're not accusing you. We're just trying to get a timeline. We need to piece together the events of the night to see if anyone saw anything that might help us find her killer."

Julie crossed her arms over her chest. "Well, I didn't see a thing. I was in my tent."

"What about earlier that day?" Jo asked. "Amber seemed to think Lynn had some kind of an appointment."

Julie frowned. "Appointment? For what?"

"We don't know. That's what we're trying to find out. Amber said Lynn was the one that wanted to come camping here in White Rock. Said she was very insistent."

Julie's gaze drifted out the window. "Yeah, actually, she did. I think she came here on vacation as a kid or something. Or maybe she had some friends here."

That caught Jo's attention. Maybe Lynn had an old score to settle and her death had nothing to do with her breakup with Noah or the company. "Friends? Who?"

Julie shook her head. "I don't know."

"So what happened that day? You all came to town for groceries and decided to do some shopping," Sam prompted.

Julie nodded. "That's right. We always do our grocery shopping together after we get to our destination. We'd arrived late the night before and gotten fast food on the way. So we headed into town." Julie frowned. "Now that I think about it, Lynn *was* acting a little anxious."

"What did she do when you got to town?"

"Whenever we go camping, we like to poke around in the local shops. Lynn collects marbles and wanted to check out the antiques store. The guys wanted to check out that Irish pub in the square there." Julie pointed out the window to O'Malley's. "We got to town just before noon and gave ourselves one hour. Then we would meet back at the pub then get groceries."

"And Lynn acted anxious?"

Julie shifted position, causing the chair to rock forward. "Sort of. Tara, Amber, and I decided to check out the secondhand store, Del's. Lynn acted kind of strange and, instead of coming with us, went to the antiques store."

"Why was that so strange?"

"Usually, we kind of hang together, but I guess Lynn was more interested in getting to the antiques store. We only had an hour."

"And you met up after you finished in the second-hand shop."

Julie's mouth twisted. "Not really. Tara isn't into used goods, and the woman in Del's told her about a boutique a few streets over, so she headed there. Amber went to get her nails done, if you can believe that. I looked for Lynn but couldn't find her. We had twenty minutes left, so I poked around in a few of the other shops until it was time to meet everyone."

"So the next time you saw Lynn was in front of O'Malley's?"

"Yes. She never said anything about any appointment. Are you sure about that?"

Jo wasn't sure. She glanced out the window, trying to picture the group. The antiques store was at the north end of the street. Lynn would've walked that way. The pub was across the green, and the men would've headed that way. The high-end shops were two streets over, so after they left Del's secondhand store, Tara would've gone down the side street to get to those. Amber would've gone right next door to get her nails done, and Julie would've been in and out of the other stores on the street. None of that told her much.

"I don't really see how any of this has anything to do with Lynn being killed. Honestly, I think you're wasting time here. No one in my group of friends would've killed her."

"That may be. But we need to establish timelines and get everyone's statement in order to determine who really did kill her. If it wasn't one of your group, then telling us everything you remember about that day will help us figure out who it was." Sam leaned across the desk toward Julie. "Is there anything else you can think of that you haven't told us?"

Julie's gaze flicked from Sam to Jo and back to Sam. The chair rocked slightly. She shook her head. "No. I think that's it."

"Okay, then you can go."

She left, and Sam looked at Jo.

"I don't think she's right about her friends. I think one of them *is* a killer," Sam said. "None of the other campers have any connection to Lynn, and there seems to be some good motives brewing here."

"Yeah. Jealousy. Greed. Maybe even revenge."

"Right. Maybe Lynn was jealous of Noah and Amber and she was killed by accident in a passionate fight with Noah."

"Or maybe Amber didn't want Noah to take up with Lynn again. Maybe Julie was right and Noah was about to get rid of Amber. If she thought he was going back to Lynn, she might have thought that making sure Lynn had a little accident would prevent that from happening."

Sam leaned back in his chair and looked out the window. "Maybe Julie doesn't know everything. Friends often hide things from each other. Maybe Noah and Lynn's breakup wasn't as amicable as he said it was. Maybe they argued about the company. Maybe Lynn's appointment had something to do with her making sure she was going to get complete control."

As usual, Jo was in sync with Sam's line of thinking. "And maybe Noah found out and wanted to stop her."

CHAPTER TWENTY-FIVE

They interviewed Dean Winters next. He was a quiet guy. Tall and handsome with that geeky computer-software look that girls sometimes went for. He was wearing shorts and sandals with white socks. It was way too early in the season for sandals up north, but Sam didn't bother to tell him that.

"Truth be told, it was a little stressful at work," Dean said in response to Sam's question about the company problems. "Money was tight, and Tara was really clamping down on spending."

Sam consulted his paperwork. "That's Tara Barrett, the chief financial officer of the company, right?"

"Yep. Tara can wring blood out of a stone. That's why she was great at the job. She could source the things we needed at half the cost." Dean shrugged. "But

I guess that wasn't enough. We were really counting on this new release."

"Tell me about the problems between Lynn and Noah," Sam said.

"There really weren't any problems. Not that I saw. Things were a little tense after they broke up, and we were all on edge with the downturn in sales, but heck, we all went camping together, right, so how many problems could there have been between them?"

"The night Lynn died. Did you see anything unusual at the campsite?"

"No." He answered way too fast, and Sam glanced at Jo. She'd noticed too.

"Are you sure? We'll find out if anything happened, and if you knew about it..." Sam let the unspoken threat hang in the air.

Dean fidgeted, and the chair wobbled back and forth. "Well, I was pretty drunk that night. I can't really say for sure what I saw. My memory's a bit fuzzy."

"Did you see someone fighting with Lynn at the party?"

"No. I actually wasn't at the campsite most of the night. There was this girl a few campsites over, and, well..." Dean shrugged. "I spent most of the night there but skedaddled out of there way before sunup. I don't know what time it was, but when I was sneaking into my tent, I'm pretty sure I saw someone else at the other end of the campsite."

"At the other end? Whose tent was at the other end?" Jo asked.

"Noah and Amber." Dean hurried on. "But I don't know who it was that I saw or even what time it was. It was just a shadow in between the tents. Could have been someone coming back from a trip to the bathroom. Heck, it could've been a bear, for all I know. It was dark, and I was still drunk. I wanted to get into my tent quickly before anyone saw me because I didn't want a lot of teasing the next day." He looked at them sheepishly. "I hope I'm not getting anyone into trouble, because I honestly can't say for sure what I saw."

"Don't worry. We'll take your condition into consideration. You've been very helpful." Sam dismissed him, and they both watched the door as he shut it.

Jo turned to Sam. "The plot thickens."

JOSHUA MOORE WAS NEXT. Since Joshua and Tara were the only other couple in the room, Jo and Sam hoped maybe they'd drunk less than the others and would have more reliable testimony.

Jo soon found out that wasn't the case.

Joshua's large frame sat slumped in the chair. He wore black cargo pants, and a white long-sleeved jersey stretched across his broad chest. He absently scratched a large welt on his neck. Mosquitos and black flies tended to love certain people, and apparently, Josh was one of them. He had several bites on his neck and arms.

"Man, I don't know what to tell you. I was pretty drunk. I passed out pretty early that night."

"So you didn't see Lynn fighting with anyone? Maybe earlier when you were in the bar?" Sam asked.

"I know Amber and Lynn got into it a little bit." Josh shrugged. "Makes sense, right? Tara would be pissed if we broke up and I showed up with another girl. But it wasn't that way with Lynn and Noah because Lynn had broken up with *him*. But Amber is not part of our group. She's a little different. More high strung. I guess maybe she didn't trust Noah or something. I've seen her and Lynn get into it a few other times, but it usually just blows over."

"What about Noah and Lynn? Did they argue?"

Josh shook his head. "Nope. It was a little awkward at work when they first broke up, but they seemed to have smoothed everything over. I didn't see any animosity between them. Honestly, man, none of us could have killed her. You don't think it was Noah or Amber, do you?"

Sam answered his question with one of his own. "What about that day when you went into town? Can you tell me what happened then?"

Josh's eyes narrowed. "Nothing happened. We went to that Irish pub over there and had a few beers. We played a game of pool. That's when we saw the other bar—that one in the church—and decided to come back later on. It looked kind of quirky, and we wanted to check it out."

"Holy Spirits?"

Josh laughed. "Yeah. That's the one. Great name."

"What did the girls do while you were playing pool?"

Josh made a face. "Heck if I know. They all went off shopping, I suppose. I know Tara came back with a bunch of stuff. She usually does."

"So you, Noah, and Dean played pool in O'Malley's, and the girls went shopping, then you met up and got groceries?"

"Yeah. Well, not exactly. Me and Dean played pool. We played against two locals. Won a hundred fifty bucks, too. But not Noah. He just sat at the bar."

"So he was at the bar the whole time you were playing?" Sam asked.

"Yeah. I mean, he was there when we went into the back where the pool tables are."

"Was he there when you came out?"

"We lost track of time and played past the time we were supposed to meet everyone. Julie came in to get us. So Noah was already outside with everyone, and then Tara came running over from the shop with her bags. For once, her usual lateness worked in our favor since it didn't make us look so bad for playing pool past the meeting time."

Jo shifted in her seat and asked, "Did Lynn mention an appointment that day?"

Josh's brow furrowed. "Appointment? No."

"So then you bought the groceries, went to the campsite, and then came back later that night to Spirits?" Jo asked.

"Yep. Well, we started drinking at the campsite then came to town." Josh's eyes widened as he realized what he'd said. "But we didn't drink and drive. Noah didn't start drinking until we got back to camp. He was the designated driver."

"At the campsite, where is your tent in relation to Noah and Amber's?" Sam asked.

"It's the next one over. Tara and I have the big one you can stand up in. Bought it new for this trip."

"After you went to bed, did you hear Noah or Amber get up?" Jo asked.

Josh made a face. "Nah. I was pretty wasted. I passed out, and I don't remember hearing a thing until some damn bird woke me up that next morning."

SAM STRETCHED IN THE CHAIR, his neck cracking, while he waited for Tara Barrett to make her way into the room. Under his desk, Lucy snored lazily. They'd have to take a break and let her outside to do her business soon. Maybe Jo could go to the diner and get her some of that pot roast Lucy seemed to like for lunch. Sam could use a plate of it himself. They'd been interviewing straight through for a few hours now, and he was glad Tara was the last one. Too bad he still had a lot of unanswered questions.

Tara perched on the edge of the chair, a pink Gucci purse balanced on her lap. Her outfit was a little trendier, less woodsy than the rest. Her pants were more formfitting, and her V-neck hot-pink tee shirt dipped low, revealing just a hint of lacy bra. She wore full makeup, and her red hair was pulled up in a waterfall style on top of her head.

Sam went through the usual questions. Tara's answers matched with everyone else's. Yes, they partied the night before. No, she didn't think anyone in the group would've killed Lynn. Of course she knew the company was in financial trouble— she was the CFO. But she felt fully confident the new release would bring them back to profitability. Everyone did, so there was no reason to kill Lynn over that. She had no idea why anyone would want her dead.

But when he got to the part about what they had done the day before when they came to town, Tara's demeanor stumbled.

"As far as I know, the boys went to that pub, and the girls went shopping." She patted her purse. "I got this.

You have a great shop on Vine Street. That's where I picked this up."

Sam knew the shop, though he'd only been in there once with his daughters. "Fern's, right?"

"Yeah, I think that's what it is."

"And Lynn went to the antiques store right at the end of Main Street, right?" Jo nodded out the window toward the main street of town.

Tara fidgeted in her seat, the chair pitching forward slightly as she followed Jo's gaze. "Is that what the others said?"

"Some of them. But some others think she might have had an appointment." Jo leaned toward her. "Would you happen to know anything about that?"

Tara's eyes flashed. "An appointment? I don't know. I wouldn't want to talk about Lynn now that she's... she's... well, you know."

Sam pushed up from his seat and came around the desk, leaning his hip on the edge so he could look down at her. "Tara. This is important. We're investigating a murder. I don't think Lynn is going to mind you talking about her if it helps us find her killer."

"Fine." Tara sighed. "I'm not sure if Lynn went to the antiques store. And I don't think she had an appointment. Not like you mean. Because I saw her meeting with someone. And that explains why she wanted to borrow my bra."

"Your bra?" Jo asked.

Sam's eyes flicked from Tara's lacey cleavage to the photos of Lynn's belongings spread across his desk. Now he knew what had bugged him about that. The bra found in her clothing pile in the woods was a fancy red lacey number, but the bras in her duffel bag were utilitarian. White cotton with a little tiny pink bow in the center. Plain Jane style, in fact, was the name of the maker.

"We borrowed each other's clothes sometimes. We were the same size." Tara's eyes filled up. "When she asked to borrow a fancy bra, I just figured she was hoping to get lucky later that night. I never suspected what she was really doing."

"What was she really doing?" Jo asked.

"Lynn might have had an appointment like you said, but it wasn't a business appointment." Tara's eyes drifted out the window. "That afternoon, I saw her meeting someone in that secluded alley near the Irish pub."

"In the alley?" Sam said. "Why would she be meeting someone there?"

Tara's eyes came back from the window to look straight at Sam. "Because she didn't want to be seen. She was meeting Noah. A *real* friendly meeting. And I don't think they were discussing business, if you get my drift."

CHAPTER TWENTY-SIX

After Tara left, Sam settled back behind his desk. Jo got up to pace the room. Lucy paced behind her.

"So Lynn had an amorous meeting with Noah in the alley," Sam said.

"But Noah was in the bar." Jo stood at the window looking out over the street. O'Malley's was two doors down from the alley where Tara had indicated she'd seen the romantic meeting between Lynn and Noah. "Then again, Derek and Josh said he was in the bar. They were playing pool, not watching Noah. He could've slipped out and met Lynn in the alley."

"But why go to all that trouble? Why the subterfuge? Why wouldn't Noah just break up with Amber and get back together with Lynn?" Sam asked.

Jo turned and paced back to Sam's desk, Lucy at her

heels. "I have no idea. People do strange things. Maybe it has something to do with her will. Maybe he was trying to be nice to get her to change it. Or maybe they had just realized they still had feelings for each other now. That could explain what Derek saw. Maybe it was Noah sneaking out to meet with Lynn."

"Or Amber sneaking out to kill her so Noah *couldn't* meet with her."

"Either way, there's something off about this," Jo said. "At least that settles the whole business of the appointment."

"Maybe. I'd still like to find out what's on her cell phone. There could be texts or phone calls that would give us a clue about something."

"Those are always interesting." Jo patted Lucy's head. "And I think we better have another talk with Noah. He forgot to tell us about his alley meeting with Lynn. But right now, I think we need to take Lucy out to do some business. And get some lunch."

Sam pushed up from his desk and walked to the door with Jo and Lucy. "Maybe we should get a leash for her."

"Why? She seems to stay right with us."

"She does, but it just seems like we should have one just in case." Sam opened the door and gestured for Jo and Lucy to proceed out into the squad room area.

Reese was at her desk. She looked up and smiled at

them. Then her eyes drifted out of the window and widened in alarm. "Oh shit! Dupont's coming."

Jo spun around. Dupont was walking up the street, clutching a manila envelope.

Jo's first inclination was to shove Lucy back into Sam's office. But what if Dupont wanted to talk to Sam privately in there? There was an entrance on the other side they never used. It opened to a small parking lot where the mail trucks used to park in back. She rushed over to the door and shoved Lucy outside just as Dupont came in the front.

"Mr. Dupont, how nice to see you." Reese's voice was light.

Dupont scowled at her. "What's going on?"

Reese smiled, all wide-eyed and innocent. "Nothing."

Dupont cleared his throat and looked at Sam. "Thank you for visiting the Palmers. It meant a lot to them."

"Of course," Sam said.

"We still need to get this solved right away. The townsfolk don't like to think of a murderer running around." Dupont's tone turned hard. "And you need to think about hiring someone. Being shorthanded has impacted this investigation."

"Not really," Sam said. "We've been working extra hours, and Kevin has been filling in for the full-time hours to take up the slack."

"And will he be taking the full-time position?"

"No, but I think it's premature to—"

Dupont shoved the manila envelope into Sam's hand. "Here are the applicants for the job. I don't want the townspeople complaining the streets aren't safe. That could reflect badly on me in the election polls next year. So I expect to be fully staffed by the end of the month." Dupont turned toward the door and shot over his shoulder, "And don't forget to keep me updated on the Palmer case."

"Man, what a jerk. He couldn't give a crap if we are understaffed or if there's crime in town—he just cares about getting reelected." Jo watched him walk away, making sure he wasn't going to come back before opening the side door to let Lucy in.

Lucy wasn't sitting on the step as Jo had expected. She looked further, in the shrubs and out into the parking lot, but Lucy was nowhere to be found. She was gone.

THE STATION FELT empty without Lucy. They had looked all around the building and into the town but didn't find her.

They were seated at Jo's desk, and Sam was eating a pastrami on rye. Jo was moving the chunks of her beef stew around in her bowl, a white bag with one last jelly donut sitting beside her. Reese munched on a salad at her own desk across the lobby. The room was filled with the smell of beef and cheese, but it was mostly silent except for their chewing. An air of sadness had descended upon them.

Kevin had come and gone. It was late afternoon, and nothing else was going on. He seemed eager to leave, so Sam had let him go home. Kevin wasn't exactly what you'd call a go-getter.

Sam glanced at the applications Dupont had given him. Maybe it was time to start looking through them.

"It might be just as well that she's gone. Eric said she might not be adoptable. If she makes the shelter circuit and no one claims her, she could be euthanized. Maybe it's better that she's out there on her own," Reese said.

Jo looked disturbed by this. She even put down the jelly donut she'd dug out of the bag and brushed off her fingers. You knew it had to be bad when Jo didn't finish her donut. "But what will she eat? In the winter, where will she sleep?"

"I don't know. It looks like she's been on her own for a while. Maybe we can look out for her somehow."

"If she sticks around the area." Sam wadded up the paper from his finished sandwich and tossed it into the trash.

Reese's computer dinged. "Good news. I ran the

password decryption program on Lynn's Google account, and looks like it worked."

"How did you know she had a Google account?" Sam asked.

Reese shrugged. "It was just a guess. A lot of people have them. You know it's free. And you can get Google calendar and email. I figured she worked for the company, and they didn't have a lot of money, so they probably didn't spend money on fancy apps."

"Did you say calendar?" Jo's attention was focused on Reese.

Reese smiled. "Yes, I did. The program figured out her password. It runs a bunch of combinations. And guess what. She *did* have an appointment that day."

Sam and Jo were across the room in a second, looking down at Reese's laptop screen. "You mean the day they all came to town, she wasn't just meeting with Noah?"

Reese tapped her finger on the screen. "That was the twelfth, right? Look at where it says, 'meeting 1 PM. R. B.'"

"R. B.?" Jo screwed up her face. "Unless R. B. is code for mauling Noah near the dumpster, it looks like Amber might have been right about Lynn being up to something."

SAM WALKED UP Main Street toward the antiques store. Julie had said she'd seen Lynn heading in that direction and that Lynn collected antique marbles. No marbles have been found in her belongings, but it was possible she didn't find anything in the store that she wanted to add to her collection.

But while Julie had said that she'd seen Lynn walk up toward the antiques store, Tara had said she'd seen her in the alley next to O'Malley's. Could she have been in both places? It was possible since they had been downtown for an hour. But what about the appointment with R. B.? Would she have had time for all three?

The bell on the antique oak door of the shop jangled as Sam opened it. Inside, Clara Weatherby looked up at him from behind the counter. She looked the same as she always did, with snow-white hair, a deeply wrinkled face, and a generous smile. Sam guessed Clara to be about eighty. She'd always owned the antique shop, and he'd known her since he was a little boy.

"Samuel! How lovely to see you. Have you decided to take up collecting? Start a collection now, and leave some family heirlooms for your lovely girls."

Sam chuckled. Antique collecting wasn't really his thing. He was more of a minimalist. "Not today, Clara. Today I have some questions."

"Hopefully, I have the answers."

"I was wondering if a tourist came in recently. A

young woman looking for marbles." Sam leaned on the glass display case Clara used as a counter while she thought.

Clara frowned. "I don't recall anything like that. And you know I have a sharp memory."

Clara's memory was legendary. If someone had come looking for a cobalt-blue Meissen teapot in 1950, she'd remember it to the day and be able to supply that teapot even if she came across it decades later. He didn't doubt that Clara would remember if Lynn had been in there.

"Did you work every day this week?" he asked. Clara had a few part-time helpers that manned the store when she went to estate sales and auctions.

"Yep. No auctions for me to attend this week, so I've been behind the counter every day. If you're asking if the girl came in this week, I can assure you she didn't."

Sam thanked Clara and left. Someone had lied about the marbles, but he didn't know if it was Julie that had lied or if Lynn had lied to Julie. Why would Lynn lie?

She clearly did have a meeting and apparently hadn't told any of her coworkers. But why keep it a secret? And who was R. B.?

Several of them had said that Lynn had headed in the direction of the antiques store. That didn't mean she stopped there, though. Maybe if he continued down the street, something would jump out at him.

Sam walked slowly, looking down the side streets

and into the shops. He wasn't just trying to figure out where Lynn might have really gone—he was also looking for any sign of Lucy.

He'd gotten attached to the dog in the short time he'd known her. He hated thinking about her trying to survive out on the streets alone. Up here, there was a lot of wildlife that could be dangerous to dogs, and winter temperatures dipped well below zero.

Reese's announcement of how Lucy could be euthanized had chilled him. Maybe Sam could find someone that would take her. One of his daughters or his ex-wife? Maybe even Mick.

At the end of the street was a plain-looking gray concrete building. In Sam's opinion, it was the ugliest building in town. It hadn't been built in the early 1900s like the rest of Main Street and didn't have the fine architectural details the other buildings had. This one had been built around 1970 and was made of giant concrete blocks that would have been more at home in an inner city than in a quaint New England town.

Sam never paid much attention to the building, and not just because of its looks. It was loaded with lawyers and accountants. He didn't get along with many lawyers in town, especially the ones that defended those who broke the law.

He was about to turn back when the black-and-gold sign listing the occupants caught his eye. One occupant in particular. Richard Bannister Funding. R. B.

CHAPTER TWENTY-SEVEN

R ichard Bannister's office was on the second
floor. Sam took the stairs. Richard was about
twelve years younger than Sam, but Sam had known
his family since he was a kid. He remembered him as a
somewhat chubby and awkward but happy kid running
around at town cookouts and riding his bike up and
down the streets.

Judging by the mahogany furniture, thick burgundy
rug, and receptionist in the foyer of his office suite,
Richard had done well for himself.

Sam wasn't wearing his police uniform, just the
windbreaker with the White Rock Police insignia, his
jeans, and a blue button-down shirt, so he flashed his
badge at the receptionist.

"Is Mr. Bannister in?"

Her eyes widened at his badge. She had nice eyes.

Light blue, with just a hint of dark mascara. Her outfit was a tailored suit. She looked worried.

"Is there some trouble?" she asked.

"Not at all." Sam introduced himself. "Sam Mason. Chief of police, but I'm sort of a family friend. Just here to ask a question or two."

Her relief was palpable. She pressed a button on the phone and announced that Sam was there.

She stood. "Right this way."

Sam followed her to a mahogany door with a large brass handle, which she opened to reveal a man in his late twenties sitting behind a gigantic desk. The awkward, chubby kid was gone. Richard had grown up to be trim and full of self-confidence. He still seemed happy.

He stood and came around the desk, extending his hand, a smile on his face. "Sam. Good to see you."

The two men shook hands. Richard didn't seem at all nervous, not that Sam expected him to be. Just because Lynn had met with him the day she died didn't mean he had anything to do with her death. Didn't mean it didn't have something to do with it either.

Sam wondered why Richard wouldn't seem a little nervous, knowing someone he'd met with had died shortly after the meeting and now the chief of police was standing in his office. Then again, maybe Richard wasn't the R. B. that had been on Lynn's calendar.

Richard gestured for Sam to sit, and he sank into a

soft, buttery leather chair that leaned back easily without squeaking. Sam wondered if he should upgrade the ancient chair in his own office as Richard sat back down behind the desk.

"I suppose this isn't just a social call," Richard said.

"Why's that?"

"You're here about Lynn Palmer, right?" Richard spun in his chair to look out the big windows that looked away from town, toward the mountains in the distance. He sucked in a breath. "Terrible thing what happened to her. We were friends in college. She was a nice girl. Smart. Do you know who did it?"

"I have some suspicions." Sam leaned forward in his chair. "So you did meet with her that day?"

"Sure." Richard shrugged. "Is that some kind of a secret?"

"Apparently. When did you meet with her?"

Richard looked down at the appointment book that lay open on his desk. "From noon until quarter to one."

"Why was she here?"

Richard looked surprised, as if Sam should've known. "She was looking to get funding for her company. Hey, look, if I was supposed to come down and tell you that I met with her, I'm sorry. I figured you would've known and come to ask if you had a question."

Sam leaned back in the chair. "Were you able to give her money?"

Richard's face darkened. "Unfortunately, I wasn't. I'm just a little guy. I don't have a lot of capital. That's why I fund the smaller companies. But I don't have extra funds to get into anything too risky, even if they do offer a high rate of return, and to tell you the truth, her company was just a bit too risky for my comfort level."

"Why's that?"

"The balance sheet. That company had way too many expenses for the income." Richard spread his hands. "I told her to tighten up expenses and come back and see me in six months." His face turned sad, and he looked down at the desk. "I guess that won't be happening now."

It made sense. The company wasn't doing well, and Lynn wanted more money. An influx of cash might help to fund a more lucrative project. But why didn't she tell any of the others? Was there someone in the company that wouldn't want her to get outside funding?

SAM WALKED SLOWLY BACK to the station, his mind turning over the particulars of the case. It made sense that Lynn was looking for funding given that sales had taken a downturn, but why had she kept it a secret?

Pedestrian traffic downtown was light, but still there was no sign of Lucy. Opening the large oak doors into the marbled foyer of the police station, he half expected to see the dog lying beside Reese's desk. But she wasn't. Somehow, the station seemed sad and empty without her.

Jo was sitting on the edge of her desk, studying the corkboard with the pictures of Lynn's belongings. She looked over at him, one brow raised. "Did you find Lucy?"

"No, but I found something else," Sam said.

"At the antiques store?"

"No. Well, I did discover that no one came in looking for marbles that day. Then, when I left the store, I noticed the sign on the ugly concrete building." Sam jerked his chin in the direction of the end of Main Street where the building jutted out from in between two others. "Richard Bannister. He does investment funding for small companies."

Jo crossed her arms over her chest. "The R. B. from her calendar?"

"One and the same." Sam told her about the conversation he'd had with Richard. "Turns out they're old friends from college, so when Lynn needed money, she looked him up."

"That's why she insisted on having the camping trip here," Jo said.

"Yep."

"So she really did have an appointment. Amber wasn't lying."

"Not about that."

Jo frowned. "But if Lynn was meeting with Richard, how could she have been in the alley with Noah?"

"It's possible. They were in town for an hour, and the meeting with Richard only lasted forty-five minutes, according to Richard. What I want to know is why didn't anyone else in the company know that she was going for funding? I think we need to ask a few more questions of our friendly campers." Sam looked around. "Where's Reese?"

Jo pointed at the door. "She stepped out to meet one of her classmates. Said he might have information on that fingerprint."

Sam frowned. "And where's Kevin?"

Jo made a show of looking at her watch. "It's six p.m. He's already gone home."

The door opened, and Reese breezed in. "I have some good news and some bad news."

"Give me the good news first," said Sam.

"The good news is my classmate was able to take your prints from the glass and run them against the partial that we found in the stolen car without logging it in officially. He logged the use in along with one of his class assignments."

"And the bad news?"

"Bad news is none of them were a match."

CHAPTER TWENTY-EIGHT

Sam and Jo had a lot to discuss with the new information and the disappointing results on the fingerprint. But Tyler's empty desk sitting in the corner was too depressing. They headed to the bar.

It was a weeknight, so Holy Spirits wasn't as crowded as it would be on the weekend. There was plenty of room up at the bar, and Jo slipped into a seat on the corner, with Sam to her right.

They ordered beers and fries. Jo thought about her fish. She'd named him Finn, and so far, he'd seemed quite happy in his little glass-bowl world on her counter. Luckily, she didn't have to rush home to feed him or let him out, as she would've if she'd had a dog.

Her chest tightened with thoughts of Lucy. Hopefully, she was doing okay out on her own. There was no way Jo could handle having a pet that required that kind of commitment right now. Having a dog would be almost like having a person that counted on her, and Jo didn't want that. Finn was plenty of responsibility for now.

"Have you looked at any of those resumes that Dupont brought over?" She dragged a french fry through a puddle of ketchup and popped it into her mouth.

Sam took a swig of his beer. "You know, I don't really feel much like hiring someone. I mean, who could replace Tyler?"

"I know what you mean, but we *are* shorthanded. Kevin doesn't want the job." Jo picked at her beer label and looked at Sam out of the corner of her eye. "If you ask me, it might be a good thing he didn't want it."

Sam leaned back in his chair, his brows tugging together. "Why do you say that?"

Jo didn't know how much she wanted to reveal. Just seeing Kevin come out of Lago when the mayor and Thorne both were inside didn't prove a thing. But she couldn't help the strange flutter in the center of her chest. It was a warning feeling that told her to be cautious around Kevin. Seemed like he was hiding something.

Then again, Jo had her own things she was hiding and wouldn't want Sam digging too closely into them. Maybe she shouldn't raise his suspicions about Kevin. His secrets might have nothing to do with their work, just as Jo's didn't. "He's just not as enthusiastic about police work as we are, or as Tyler was."

Sam nodded and hunched back over his beer. "Yeah, I know what you mean."

Mick slipped into the seat around the corner of the bar next to Sam. No sooner had his butt hit the leather chair than a drink appeared in front of him. He really had Billie trained.

Mick leaned toward Jo and Sam. "Did you run the print?"

"Yeah. Bad news. It didn't match."

"It didn't?" Mick pressed his lips together and shook his head. "I know there's something funny going on there. It just adds up. The woman has a grandson into drugs. Drugs are found in the car. There's got to be a connection." He downed his drink in one swallow. "What about your other case? You guys look pretty down in the dumps. Things not going good?"

"Got a few new leads. But they're confusing." Sam took another swig.

"Anything I can help with?" Mick reached across Sam and snagged a fry. Sometimes they used Mick when they needed to get information that they couldn't acquire in their official capacity, but with the Palmer case, Jo knew they couldn't risk anything that wasn't on the up and up. Not at this point.

Sam shook his head.

"What about your girlfriend?" Mick asked.

Jo almost choked on a fry. Sam had a girlfriend? She coughed and punched her fist in the center of her chest where a strange pang had surfaced.

"When did you find time to get a girlfriend?" She hoped her voice sounded casual. It wasn't that she minded Sam having a girlfriend. Not as if she was jealous or anything. But, somewhere deep down inside, she was afraid a girlfriend might change their work friendship. And her work friendship with Sam was about all she had in the way of human relationships. She really needed to get out more.

Mick stood and slapped some money on the bar. "Yeah, she's a real looker too. Brown eyes, black-and-brown hair, four nice legs. She could use a little shave, though."

"Oh, you mean Lucy." Jo laughed. "Have you seen her tonight? She ran off from the police station earlier today."

"Haven't seen her, but I'll keep an eye out," Mick said. "In the meantime, I'm going to dig a little further into this Bartles kid. I know there's a connection."

"Thanks, Mick," Sam said as Mick sauntered out of the bar.

Sam finished his beer and signaled for another. Jo pushed the basket of fries to him and swiveled her chair to face out into the bar, her elbows on the bar top, feet swinging slightly in front of her.

The bar was mostly empty. Two couples sat in the

pews at one of the long tables near the door, burgers loaded up with specialty fixings in front of them. Jo could smell sautéed onions and figured one of them must have ordered the Alps Burger. It was her favorite, smothered in sautéed onions and Swiss cheese.

A couple sat at one of the round tables, their chairs pushed close together. Two tables over, four local guys sat with beers in front of them. Jo knew them all.

"The Palmer case is getting stranger and stranger. Why didn't Lynn tell anyone she was meeting with Richard? And what about her phone? Did the killer throw that in the river because there might be evidence on it, or did it fall in by accident?" she asked.

"Good question. Maybe if we ever get the information from Verizon, we'll find out if there was something else on there the killer might not want anyone to know about." Sam ate a fry.

"What if the killer wanted to hide the fact that she had that appointment or hide any calls or texts between her and Richard? They might not have realized she used an online app to schedule the appointment or that we could get her phone information from her cell phone carrier."

"Lots of people don't know about that. Doesn't help us narrow things down."

Jo turned back facing the bar and picked at her beer label some more. It had gotten nice and soggy and peeled off easily. "Sure do have a lot of things to puzzle over. There's the meeting with Richard."

"And there's Tara seeing Lynn with Noah right around the same time."

"And Noah and Amber were both acting sketchy about where they were the night of Lynn's death."

"And Lynn borrowed Tara's bra?" Sam scrunched up his face and looked at Jo. "Do girls do that? And why would she want a fancy bra if she wasn't having a fling with Noah?"

Jo had never had a girlfriend that she was close enough to to borrow a bra from. "Some girls borrow each other's clothes all the time. I guess bras would be no exception. But Lynn might not have borrowed it because of Noah. Maybe there was someone else."

"True. And let's not forget Derek saw someone at Noah's tent that night. Could have been Noah sneaking out to meet Lynn."

"Or Amber." Jo leaned over the bar and fished behind it for another ketchup bottle, which she found exactly where she knew Billie kept it. She twisted off the cap and smacked the bottom until a blob oozed out onto the side of the french fry basket.

"Julie was the one that said she saw Lynn going to the antiques store, but Lynn never went there. Why would Julie say that?"

"Maybe Lynn just told her that's where going and Julie assumed. Lynn would've had to head in that direction, and if she didn't want anyone to know about the meeting with Richard, then she probably just *told* them she was going to the antiques store."

"Something doesn't add up. Why wouldn't Noah know that Lynn was meeting Richard for the financing? We need to talk to Noah. My guess is he's smack dab in the center of this."

Jo crunched down on a lukewarm ketchup-covered fry. "He does benefit directly from Lynn's death with getting the extra shares of the stock."

"Maybe the financing would have diluted his stock," Sam said. "They would have had to give Richard some shares in the company. Maybe Lynn did tell Noah about it. Maybe he didn't want it. He might really have been meeting Lynn that day and lied about it to cover up that he knew she was seeking financing."

"Seems like he had a good motive, but there might be more to the story, and we need to talk to Lynn's friends again, because Noah's not the only one in that group that's telling lies."

CHAPTER TWENTY-NINE

S
am drove out to the campground first thing the next morning. The early-morning sun filtered through the leaves, giving the air a golden glow. Just beyond the campground, the river gurgled. Sam battled a swarm of black flies as he approached the campsite.

On the picnic table, Tara was preparing lunches. Jars of peanut butter and jelly sat on the table along with the six waterproof lunch sacks. Something about that bugged Sam. Their friend was dead, and they were going about business as usual. Didn't seem right.

Derek, who was backing out of his tent with a backpack, looked around at him quizzically. Tara stopped spreading jelly.

Julie finished spraying her arm with the bug spray and tossed the can to Sam, who spritzed himself.

Noah turned from the makeshift clothesline where

he was taking down some pants. "Chief Mason? Have you found who... who did that to Lynn?"

"Not yet. But I have some interesting news." They'd all gathered closer to the picnic table, and Sam put his foot up on the bench, resting his arm on his knee and bending forward slightly.

"Seems that Lynn had seen an investor in town. She was trying to get more funding for the company. Did you all know that?" Sam studied the faces. They all seemed surprised. Thing was, he knew that at least a few of them were accomplished liars, and he couldn't tell if they had already known and were covering, or if they were truly surprised.

"She never said anything to me, but we didn't normally discuss company finances. I was just a programmer," Julie said. "Was that the appointment she had?"

Sam nodded then turned to Tara. "What about you? You're the CFO, aren't you?"

Tara shrugged, slowly screwing the top back on the peanut butter. "I didn't know anything about it. You mean she saw someone here in town?"

Sam nodded then turned his gaze on Noah. Amber stepped a little closer to Noah, glancing up at him uncertainly. "What about you, Noah? You guys owned the company together. Surely she would've discussed this with you?"

"She didn't. That can't be true. I'm sure she would

have told me." Noah did look confused, but he could be an accomplished liar.

Sam slid his foot off the bench and stood. "Lynn getting financing could cause a problem, right?"

"Why would it cause a problem?" Noah asked quickly. His posture turned defensive. "We needed money. Nobody's made that a secret. And what does this have to do with her death, anyway? Why are you acting like you suspect us? We're her friends—none of *us* did it."

Sam wasn't anywhere near sure of that, but it was never good to tip your hand. He simply nodded slightly then looked at Noah. "Maybe it would be better if we talked further over there." He jerked his head toward the Tahoe.

Noah's eyes darted around to the others, then he broke from the pack and headed toward the Tahoe.

They leaned against the front of the car, Sam placing himself so that he could see Noah as well as the others at the campground. He didn't know who was lying, and he wanted to see their reactions to him taking Noah out and talking to him privately. If one of them had something to hide, they might show it in their actions.

"Does Amber know you were getting back together with Lynn?" Sam asked.

"What?" Noah's face scrunched up. "I wasn't getting back together with Lynn." He glanced back at the crowd nervously.

Amber was watching them, practically craning her neck to be able to overhear. Tara had gone back to making sandwiches. Derek and Jason were sitting at the table, and Julie was stuffing the bug spray into her backpack.

"Really? One of your friends over there saw you in a compromising position with her in the alley in town the day she was killed," Sam said.

"What? Who said that? That's crazy! I was in O'Malley's pub with Derek and Josh."

"So you said. But Derek and Josh were playing pool and can't swear that you were actually in the pub the whole time."

Noah pushed his hands through his sandy-colored hair. "I was there. Why would I meet with Lynn? We broke up a long time ago."

"Really?" Sam said. "That's funny, because Derek says he saw someone sneaking around your tent the night Lynn was killed. Amber seemed a little uncertain when she verified you had been in the tent all night."

Noah's eyes shifted to the left, his jaw tightening.

Sam continued. "So when someone else said they saw you with Lynn in the alley, and given the fact that you are benefiting from her death by getting all the shares of the company, I figured you must've known she was going for financing. Then I figured maybe getting financing was a double-edged sword for you. It would water down your shares, but your company needed it to survive. Then again, if Lynn was out of the way and you owned all the shares, the watering down might not be so bad."

Noah's face showed increasing stages of horror as Sam relayed this information.

Sam kept going. He wasn't entirely convinced Noah was the killer, but Noah was lying about something, and Sam wanted to see if he could scare the truth out of him. "The way I figure it is that you *did* meet with Lynn. Maybe first you were trying to smooth-talk her out of the financing. But when that didn't work, you had to take more drastic measures. Derek *did* see you that night. You snuck out of your tent and did what you had to do to protect your interests."

"No!" Noah shook his head vehemently. Glancing back at the group again, he stepped closer to Sam. "I wasn't meeting with Lynn. But it is true that I wasn't in my tent. Don't tell anyone, but I—"

The radio in the Tahoe squawked noisily to life, interrupting Noah's confession. Sam had turned his phone off just so he wouldn't get interrupted. He'd told Reese to call only if there was a dire emergency. He went around to the driver's-side door to grab the receiver, when Reese's panicked voice rang out, chilling his blood. "Sam. Emergency. There's been a dog hit down by the Pembroke Bridge."

Sam's heart jerked. Lucy? He grabbed the mic and pressed the button. "German shepherd?"

"Sounds like it. Driver said she was still alive. You better get there fast."

Screw Noah. He would catch up with him later. Might be a good idea to let him stew on what Sam had told him, anyway. Better yet, if he told the others, the real killer might do something stupid and reveal themselves.

Right now, Sam's quick actions might be the only thing that kept Lucy alive. He jumped into the Tahoe, flicked on the siren and lights, and screeched out of the campground toward the Pembroke Bridge.

CHAPTER THIRTY

Sam screeched to a halt behind the old 1970s station wagon that was listing into the ditch on the side of the road with its flashers on. He jumped out of the Tahoe, bracing himself for the worst as he ran around to the front of the car.

There was no dog lying in the road.

"She just came out of nowhere!" a balding man, his belly protruding over his belt, pacing in front of his car with a worried look on his face, said. "I hope she's not hurt badly."

"Was it a big dog? Looked like a German shepherd and mixed with something big?" Sam asked.

The man nodded and pointed to the guardrail that ran along the road just before the bridge. "She ran off over there."

Beyond the guardrail, the Sacagewassett River

flowed by at a fast clip. If Lucy had fallen into the river, she was probably already gone. Sam vaulted over the guardrail and scrambled down the embankment, rocks clattering into the river as he went.

A high-pitched whine sounded to his left. Lucy was sitting next to a pile of debris that had accumulated at a bend in the river. Relief washed over him. She was sitting upright, so hopefully, she hadn't been hurt too badly. He didn't see any blood, but the lack of obvious external injuries didn't mean that she didn't have potentially fatal internal injuries. He'd better get her to the vet right away.

Sam squatted to her level. "Are you okay?"

Lucy trotted over, her brown eyes looking up at him. Sam checked her over, running his hands down her sides, her legs, and her chest. He didn't find any injuries except a small tear in her right ear.

"What happened? Did the car clip you here?" Sam asked.

"Woof!" Lucy broke away and trotted toward the debris.

"Hey, come back. I want to take you to the vet to get you looked after."

Lucy whined. Maybe she'd been hurt more than he thought. Maybe he could bribe her into going to the vet. "If you come with me, I'll get you one of Billie's burgers."

Lucy trotted up to Sam, nudged his hand, and then

trotted back to the debris. She wasn't hurt. She was trying to tell him something.

Sam went over to the pile. There were empty soda bottles, cans, plastic bags, even part of a grocery cart. Sam hated to see the trash. He remembered a time when there was hardly any, but now the more people that came, the more trash there was.

Lucy was sniffing at something in the pile. It was soaking wet and filthy with dirt, but Sam could see it had once been white. The little pink bow on it was hanging by a thread. A jolt kicked his chest. Sam reached into the debris and picked it up. The maker was Plain Jane.

"Sam? What the hell are you doing?"

Sam squinted up at Jo, who was standing at the top of the rock embankment. She must've heard the call for the accident and rushed down. She had her sunglasses off and a quizzical look on her face. Her eyes flicked from the bra to Sam.

He turned to face her, the bra dripping from his hand.

"I think Lucy just solved the case."

CHAPTER THIRTY-ONE

Jo took care of calming down the driver and sending him on his way while Sam brought Lucy to the vet. Lucy had only been grazed by the car, the tear in her ear the only injury. Sam called Reese with the good news and told her to assemble the campers in his office in two hours. He had a few things to check into first.

By the time they gathered in his office, it was just past noon. The campers sat nervously in extra chairs they'd brought in from the squad room. Lucy was out in the lobby, being fed a sumptuous meal of steak and carrots. Apparently, she preferred that to sitting in on Sam's big reveal.

Jo sat off to the side, her notepad in her lap, the eraser end of her pencil tapping on it rhythmically.

Kevin was in the room too. He stood silently by the

door in his blue police uniform, his arms crossed over his chest in an intimidating manner. The campers kept glancing at him. It all added to setting them on edge, which was exactly the way Sam wanted them to feel. He knew the more nervous they got, the more apt they were to turn on each other.

Sam came around to the front of his desk, leaning his backside on it and looking down at the campers in their seats.

"Did you find out who killed Lynn?" Derek looked around at his friends and back up at Sam. "I mean, that's why you called us here, right?"

"That's right," Sam said. "Some new evidence has come to light, and I think I know exactly what happened the night Lynn died."

Sam walked back behind his desk, where they had taped up all the pictures from the investigation on a giant corkboard. There were pictures of the pile of Lynn's clothes they had found in the woods, pictures of the contents of her duffel bag and what they'd found in her tent, and even pictures of her body as they'd found it in the river, which Sam noticed the girls studiously avoided looking at.

Sam pointed to the picture of the pile of clothing. "Lynn was wearing these clothes the night she died. But, for some reason, she took them off. To go swimming in the middle of the night? We didn't think so." He turned to face the campers. "Our theory was that she was meeting a lover. Something went wrong, and he killed her, then dragged her body down into the river and sent it downstream, hoping it would look like an accident."

"I knew it! It was that guy from the bar," Amber said.

Sam shook his head and pointed to a picture of a receipt. "No. That guy had an alibi. He was pumping gas at almost the exact time that Lynn was killed. There was no way he could've killed her, dragged her body to the river, and then run back to his car and driven to the gas station."

Their eyes flicked from the receipt to Sam's face. Julie spoke up. "Well, then it must've been someone else at the campground."

Sam stared at her. "Really? Was there someone else there? I talked to each of you, and no one mentioned anyone else with Lynn."

They shifted in their seats and looked at each other uneasily. "There were some other campers that we talked to a little, but I don't remember anyone else *with* her," Josh said.

"Me either," Derek added.

"But wait a minute. If it wasn't anyone else, that means it was one of us." Julie's eyes shifted around the group nervously.

"Precisely," Sam said. "Now, imagine our surprise when we discovered that Lynn had something in her will set up so that Noah would get her shares in the company. A fact that Noah conveniently forgot to tell us."

All heads turned toward Noah. His cheeks flushed crimson. "Of course she had that in her will. We agreed on that from the start. It wasn't a secret. I just didn't think it was important. That's why I never mentioned it. I didn't even think about it, actually."

"Well, it meant that you would gain from her death," Sam said. "And since she was trying to get financing for the company, maybe you either didn't want the financing or maybe, if she didn't tell you about it as you claim, she was going behind your back to gain a broader control of the company. You'd broken up, so why would she want to share control with you? Maybe she wanted it all for herself."

The room was silent.

"That's why I was so confused when someone saw you and Lynn in a compromising position the day she died," Sam continued.

Amber made a squeaking noise and shot a look at Noah.

"I told you, I wasn't with Lynn. I was in the bar!" Noah started to get out of his chair, but a warning look from Kevin had him sitting back down quickly.

"Too bad no one can corroborate that. Derek and Josh had their eyes on the pool game. They can't say for sure that you really were in the bar." Sam walked the length of the whiteboard, looking at the pictures slowly. Then he turned to face them again. "And Derek saw someone by your tent at almost the same time Lynn was killed."

Everyone was quietly staring at Noah.

"In fact, we know Lynn was planning on meeting someone because she borrowed a fancy bra from Tara." Sam pointed to the red bra in the pile of clothes they'd found in the woods. "And when I took the statements from you and Amber, I had a sneaky suspicion that each of you was lying about being in that tent."

Amber turned on Noah. "You snuck out to meet her? How *could* you?"

Sam raised a brow at Noah. "So you weren't in the tent? Where were you? Did you sneak down to the beach with Lynn and kill her so that you could get control of the company?"

Noah shook his head frantically. "No! I wasn't with Lynn. I swear!" His eyes drifted over to Julie.

"That's right. He wasn't," Julie said softly. "He was in *my* tent with me. He couldn't have killed Lynn."

The others gasped, but Sam wasn't surprised. He stood in front of Julie, arms crossed over his chest. "And you're willing to swear to this? Why didn't you tell me before?"

"Yes. Of course." Julie looked at the others apologetically. "We didn't want anyone to know. Things just sort of happened, and Noah wanted to let Amber down gently. We didn't want to tell anyone yet because things were so awkward after Noah and Lynn broke up."

Sam looked at Amber. "That's why you faltered when we asked if you and Noah were both in the tent for the rest of the night, isn't it? You knew Noah wasn't in the tent."

Amber looked down at the floor. "Yes. I didn't know where he was, and I didn't want to think that he could kill Lynn. But I wasn't gonna be the one to get him in trouble." She sniffed then scooted her chair away from Noah and fixed him with an angry glare. "Now I wish I *did* tell you."

Sam nodded slowly then turned to Derek. "And you saw someone at the tent, but you didn't know what time it was. It could've been Noah sneaking off to Julie's tent or slinking back to his own, couldn't it?"

Derek shrugged. "I'm sorry. I just wasn't looking at my watch or anything, so I have no idea. I was sneaking around myself."

"Then it could have been Amber, right?" Sam asked.

"Hey, now wait a minute!" Amber shot out of her chair. "I might have lied about Noah being in the tent, but I was in there the whole time. Why would I kill Lynn?"

"Jealousy?" Sam said then held his palm up. "Don't worry. Now that we know Noah was meeting with Julie, we know it's unlikely that you were the killer. If you'd left the tent to follow him, you would have seen him with Julie, and then you'd have no reason to kill Lynn." Sam made a motion for Amber to sit back down.

"Right." Amber sat.

Sam walked back over to the whiteboard. "Seems like there was a lot of sneaking around and lying going on with you people."

They shifted restlessly in their chairs.

"The day you all went into town, Julie said Lynn went to the antiques store."

"She did." Julie seemed mad.

"She collected antiques. Marbles," Noah said.

"But she didn't go there. She went to see Richard Bannister about financing," Sam said.

"So this Richard Bannister guy was the lover she met that night on the beach where you found her clothes?" Josh asked.

"There was no lover. We think she was fully clothed and the killer took her clothes off after they killed her." Sam pointed to the picture of Lynn's pants that clearly showed the tear in the fabric. "That's how her pants got ripped. It's not easy to get clothes off a dead body. The pants must have gotten ripped in the struggle. But the killer needed to get the clothes off and pile them up to make us think she met a lover. They even left a little extra piece of clothing there to seal the deal... or because they had to."

Josh made a face. "They *had* to? What do you mean?"

Sam pointed to the picture of the bra he'd fished out of the river. "I found this downstream yesterday. It happens to be the same exact size and make of bra that we found in Lynn's duffel bag."

Amber scrunched up her face. "So what? A lot of people wear the same make and size of bra."

Sam crossed his arms over his chest. "Sure, but this one had Lynn's initials on it."

"But she was dragged into the river in her under-wear. Her bra probably came off and floated down-stream," Derek said.

"I'm sure it did." Sam turned back to the whiteboard and pointed again at the picture of the pile of clothing. "But how many people wear *two* bras?"

"What?"

"See, we found a bra in the pile of clothing, too." Sam tapped the picture that showed the bra. "Derek's right, though, the bra did come off when the killer was putting her in the river. It couldn't have been easy to drag her in deep enough so she would float in the current. The bra must have come unhooked and floated away before the killer noticed. And that presented a problem for the killer."

"How so?" Josh asked. "I mean, the bra could have come off while she was meeting this supposed lover."

"True," Sam said. "Except the killer's initial plan was to pretend that Lynn died by accident. It was a pretty good plan, too. Everyone knew that Lynn swam alone at night. She'd been drinking, so it was plausible that she could have gone for a swim, slipped and hit her head, then died in the river. If her death had been ruled an accident as the killer planned, there would have been no investigation, and the killer would have gotten off scot-free."

Sam paused, watching them as it sank in.

"The problem was that everyone knew that Lynn swam in just her underwear. So if she took her clothes off to go for a swim, that pile would have a bra in it. In fact, the absence of a bra would be suspicious. So the killer did something she probably thought was very clever. She put one of her own bras into the pile. Later on, when things didn't go according to plan and the death was ruled as a murder, she even used that as part of her plan B—to make it look like Lynn was meeting a lover." Sam turned to Tara. "She even told us she'd loaned Lynn the bra herself."

Tara sucked in a breath. "I did. I wasn't lying. Why would I want to kill Lynn?"

"Ahh... That is the question. I'll get to that." Sam went back to the whiteboard. "Julie said she'd seen Lynn going to the antiques store the day you all went into town."

"She told me that's where she was going," Julie said. "When I saw her head in that direction, I just assumed..."

"Right. But she wasn't going to the antiques store. I

checked. Her real destination was at the end of the street. Because at the end of the street was an old friend of hers, Richard Bannister. He invests in small companies like yours."

"But why would she be secretive about that? Why not tell us?" Noah asked.

Sam had wondered about that himself. "That, I do not know. Maybe she was afraid the funding wouldn't go through and she didn't want to get people's hopes up. But there was one person here who I think already knew the funding wouldn't go through. Isn't that right, Tara?"

"I don't know what you're talking about." Tara looked at her friends imploringly. "He's making this up. He's just trying to pin this murder on me so that he can close the case."

Sam ignored her. "When Tara's plan to make the death look like an accident didn't work, she tried to blame Jesse. And when she found out he had an alibi, she tried to implicate Noah. She said in her statement that she saw Lynn and Noah kissing in the alley next to O'Malley's."

Noah let out an exasperated sigh. "For the millionth time, I was *not* meeting Lynn."

"I know that." Sam pointed at the picture of another receipt. "She couldn't have seen you meeting Lynn in the alley because she was three streets over, buying a purse."

"I saw them before that!" Tara was becoming irate, exactly as Sam had planned. People always said too much when they got pissed off.

"The timing doesn't match," Sam said. "Lynn's meeting with Bannister was from twelve until twelve forty-five. So she couldn't have been meeting Noah then."

"It was after that." Tara spat the words out. Sam noticed everyone was leaning away from her.

"You couldn't have seen them," Sam said. "According to Julie, you left the secondhand store around twelve forty and went to Fern's. You were on foot, so it takes about five minutes. But Fern's is two streets over. You can't see the alley next to O'Malley's from there. And Josh said you were meeting them. You rushed over from Fern's, and everyone was already gathered on the sidewalk."

Noah narrowed his eyes at Tara. "Tara, is this true? Why would you do this?"

Tara's eyes darted back and forth between all her friends. They all had strange looks on their faces, as if they were starting to see that what Sam was saying made sense. The clues were starting to sink in, and she wasn't going to be able to wriggle her way out of this. He gave the final blow.

"Tara had a reason. When Lynn met with Richard, he told her he couldn't give your company more financing because your expenses were too high for your income. But I think the truth was, if you look at the company books, you'll see some of those expenses were overinflated." Sam tapped the receipt from Fern's. "Tara had expensive tastes, like this three-hundred-dollar purse." He gestured to her outfit. "She's wearing expensive camping gear, and I noticed her backpack on the first day, as it's a very expensive model."

"I don't have to listen to this!" Tara tried to get out of her chair, but Josh held her arm, his fingers making white marks in her flesh.

"I think you do. We all do." Josh's voice was tinged with sadness.

"Naturally, after Lynn talked to Richard, she would have approached Tara. She's the CFO. She would know about the finances."

"Tara never said anything about that." Noah looked at Josh. "Did she say anything to you?"

Josh shook his head sadly.

"Of course she didn't," Sam said. "Tara couldn't have an audit happening. She was embezzling from the company."

"Now, wait a minute," Noah said. "If Lynn knew about that, she would have told me."

"I don't think Lynn knew. But if she wanted the financing, they would have to scrutinize expenses. So she must have mentioned that to Tara, and it must have been that night. It was probably the only time she had her alone after she talked to Richard. Maybe she still didn't want to tell the rest of you until she was sure of what would happen with the financing."

Tara must have been out of excuses—she sat there silently.

Sam continued. "I'm not sure how it happened. I imagine Tara tried to talk her out of doing an audit, and Lynn insisted. Maybe Tara snuck up on her later that night in the woods, or maybe she lured her there. Or maybe Lynn didn't mention the audit until that night when they were on the beach and it erupted into an argument. Tara hit her with a rock on the beach and killed her then pulled her clothes off to make it look like she had an accident while swimming. But her bra must have floated away, and her pants got snagged. Tara shoved her in the river, tossed the phone in after her, then folded up her clothes and added her own bra so no one would notice one article of clothing was missing. Isn't that right, Tara?"

Tara dissolved into tears. "I didn't mean any harm. I was just borrowing the money. I was gonna pay it back when we released the new game and were all rolling in the dough."

She looked up at her friends through her tears, begging them to believe her, but now they were all pushing their chairs back away from her. "I didn't mean to kill her, but she accused me, and we argued, and then we started fighting. The next thing I knew, I had smashed her with a rock. I had to do something. So I pushed her into the water, hoping it would look like an accident. I threw the phone in too so no one would see if she had calls from that finance guy."

Josh buried his face in his hands. The others looked stunned.

"No. I don't believe it." Noah looked at Tara in disgust. "And you tried to blame it on me?"

"Unfortunately, we have the evidence to prove it. And now a confession." Sam nodded to Kevin, and he went over to Tara, taking her elbow, gently lifting her from the chair. He read her her rights as he walked her out of the room.

CHAPTER THIRTY-TWO

K evin glanced in the rearview mirror at the redhead in the backseat of the police car. She'd cried for a while at first but was quiet now, looking out the window. Accepting her fate.

The White Rock police station was too small to keep anyone overnight. They only had one cell, and it was used rarely. Mostly for drunks to sleep it off. But this girl would be locked up until she could go before a judge, and Sam had asked him to drive her to the county jail. Sam had never asked him to do that before —usually he relied on Jo or Tyler.

Sam had never asked him to sit in on an interrogation before, either. Pride warred with regret in Kevin's chest. Did Sam trust him and want him to be part of the team?

Would Kevin's little side job put that in jeopardy?

Watching Sam get the redhead to confess had been interesting. He admired the way Sam went about it. Forcing her hand into admitting she'd done it. Kevin could learn a lot from Sam, and it had felt good to be in on things for once instead of sitting on the sidelines.

And now he felt guilty because passing along that information he'd been paid to look for felt like spying on Sam and Jo. It felt like a betrayal.

The information wasn't anything that would hurt Sam or Jo. It was just general stuff. Stuff that might help them, or at least that was what Kevin wanted to think. Especially if Sam and Jo weren't doing anything wrong. And he was pretty sure they weren't.

But if his contact was right and Sam and Jo and Tyler had been a part of something that wasn't on the up and up, then he didn't want to be an insider in their little club. It was his duty to expose that, right?

Something sharp unfurled in his chest, obliterating his earlier cozy feelings of inclusion. He wasn't really sure who wanted that information. The large sum of money he'd been offered had been enough for him to accept with no questions asked. But he had to wonder if the sheriff's department or state police would be paying him so much money. Did they even pay officers on the side like that? Heck, he hadn't even really given them much information yet at all, and they still kept sending money.

The redhead's sorrowful sniffle caught his attention, and he looked in the rearview mirror again. According to what he'd heard in Sam's office, the girl had screwed over her friends. And now she looked miserable. She'd lost her friends and her freedom. Kevin just hoped what he'd done wouldn't end with similar consequences.

AFTER KEVIN HAULED TARA AWAY, the campers sat in Sam's office in disbelief. None of them had wanted to believe they had a killer in their midst. Sam wasn't surprised—you never knew what was lurking around underneath the surface when it came to people. When they finally left, they said they were planning to pack up and head home. None of them had any enthusiasm for camping.

Reese had just taken Lucy out for a walk when Kevin came back. The three of them leaned against Jo's desk, coffee mugs in hand. Jo passed around the donut bag.

"So I was wondering. How did finding the bra in the river help you figure things out?" Kevin asked.

Sam thought he saw something flicker in the officer's eyes that he hadn't seen before. Interest. Sam realized that was one of the reasons he'd never really taken to Kevin. He'd never seemed interested in the cases. Until now. Maybe it was because Sam had never included him as he had in the office here. Might be a smart idea to include him more often.

"Actually, I should've figured it out earlier. When we were at the campsite after we discovered the body, Tara was making lunches for the campers. She only had six lunches," Sam said.

"So? They were going hiking, right? Makes sense they would be making lunches," Kevin said.

"Sure. Except there were seven campers. Why was Tara only making six lunches? Because she knew one of the campers wouldn't be joining them."

"Why even make the lunches?" Jo asked. "She had to have known that Lynn would be discovered missing. Even if the body washed downriver and wasn't found, they wouldn't have gone hiking if she was missing."

Sam shrugged. "Keep up appearances, I guess. She couldn't very well refuse to make the sandwiches. Then everyone would know something was up. She must have been not thinking straight and subconsciously not made one for Lynn since she knew Lynn wouldn't be eating lunch that day."

Jo squeezed her donut in the middle, causing a blob of jelly to poke out of the hole. She swiped at it with her finger then licked it off. "Yeah, but there was no motive for Tara. At least not that we could figure, so why would we be scrutinizing everything she did? I wouldn't beat myself up for not noticing that."

"The signs were there. Company doing badly. Tara was the CFO." Sam chewed his donut thoughtfully. "She was very clever, though. When her initial plan of making it look like an accident didn't work, she adapted pretty quickly. Like how she told us that Lynn borrowed her bra. She knew she put it in the pile. Probably, no one would have noticed that if Lynn's death had been ruled accidental, but with us asking questions, she was afraid it might come up, and telling us Lynn borrowed it was the perfect way to explain it being there."

"Not to mention it gave her extra ammunition to push her lie about Lynn and Noah," Jo said.

"Too bad she didn't know we could get Lynn's phone records." Kevin held up a sheet of paper that was on his desk. "Verizon finally came through, and Lynn *had* made calls to Roger Bannister. We would've tracked him down eventually and found out about the company's troubles."

"Yeah, Reese really helped speed things up with that one." Jo looked at Sam pointedly. "She might be a little green, but I think she's a great asset to the team."

"Agreed. Maybe we should give her more to do." Sam glanced at the piles of resumes that were still on the corner of Jo's desk. "I suppose we still have to hire someone new, though."

He glanced at Kevin just in case the officer had

changed his mind about coming on full time. Kevin looked away.

The door opened, and Dupont entered. Instead of his usual scowling face, he looked almost jovial.

"Congratulations on solving the Palmer case! This is wonderful news." He clapped Sam on the back, and Sam nodded and stepped away. He still didn't trust Dupont and didn't need his praise.

"I hope it brings some closure to her parents," Sam said.

"I've talked to them. They are relieved. Of course, they're upset that it was a friend of Lynn's but glad that justice will be done." Dupont glanced over at Tyler's desk and back at Sam. "How are the new hires coming along?"

"We've been kind of too busy solving this case to interview people, but now that it's over, I guess I'll have to start weeding through the resumes." Sam put the donut down. Suddenly, he didn't have an appetite.

"Good. I want to make sure this town is in tiptop shape. Show the citizens that I keep crime to a minimum here and that I'm the best man for the job of mayor," Dupont said.

Across from Sam, Kevin's eyes widened. He was facing the door, and Sam turned around too late to see Reese coming in with Lucy. Lucy saw Dupont and growled, her hackles rising.

Dupont whirled around.

"Have you people been keeping this dog here?" He jerked his head back in Sam's direction. "I thought I told you to get rid of her. It won't do to have dogs in the police station. I'm running for reelection, and I can't have any blemish on my reputation."

Sam didn't give a crap about Dupont's reputation and was about to say so when Reese cut in.

"Oh, don't worry about that, Mayor Dupont," Reese said.

"Don't give me any bullshit about bringing her to the shelter. You people have told me that twice already. Now, I want to tell you there are no—"

"It's not that," Reese interrupted him, but in the nicest way possible. She went over to her computer and hit a few keys. The printer hummed to life and spit out a page. Reese grabbed it and held it up. "I thought you knew. We've been accepted for a K-9 LEAP grant. Lucy is an official K-9 dog now."

Dupont ripped the paper out of Reese's hand and glowered at it. "K-9 program? That costs the town money. I don't remember authorizing this."

"Actually, it's a grant. It won't cost any taxpayer money from the town. In fact, I've talked to a bunch of people in town, and they are very impressed with how you were able to get this extra resource for the town without having to raise taxes." Reese smiled at Dupont. "Very clever of you."

Dupont's demeanor faltered. "They are?"

"Yes. Everyone knows that Lucy was instrumental in solving this last murder. Having her here as a resource will be a great asset to the town and help keep crime levels low."

Dupont cleared his throat. "Well, I see what you mean."

He looked down at Lucy and held a tentative hand out toward her. The dog eyed him suspiciously but gave his hand an obligatory sniff.

"Very well, then." Dupont tapped his lips with his finger. "Maybe this is something I should play out in my campaign. People like dogs, right?"

"Absolutely, they do," Reese said.

"Good. Well, carry on." Dupont exited, and Jo turned back to Reese.

"What was that all about? Did you make that up?"

Reese laughed. "No. Remember the other day when we were talking and you said it was too bad we couldn't hire Lucy?"

"Yeah, but I was joking."

"That got me thinking. I know other precincts have K-9 dogs, and I did some research and asked around at school. It turns out there's a grant program. So I took the initiative to apply." Reese looked sheepishly at Sam. "I hope you don't mind me doing it without asking, but you were busy with the case, and I figured it was a long shot, so I didn't want to get anyone's hopes up."

"I don't mind at all. But how did you get it past the mayor's office? Don't they have to sign off on this?" Sam asked.

"Sure they do, but I have a friend that works in city hall, and she just happened to put the paperwork in along with a bunch of other paperwork, and Henley Jamison, the vice mayor, rubber-stamped it. Then I have another friend who's really good with computers, and we managed to, um... fast-track the application."

Sam narrowed his gaze. "Fast-track? How did you do that?"

Reese grimaced. "Well, I—"

Sam held up his palm. "Never mind. I don't want to know. The important thing is you got it done."

Reese beamed. "Now Lucy can be here officially all day. We don't have to bring her to the shelter. She could stay here in the cell, or someone can take her home at night. And she won't be alone all day while we're at work. Plus, she really did help out. The grant pays for dog food, a bulletproof dog vest, even a dog bed."

"Excellent work." Sam squatted down, and Lucy trotted over. Maybe it was his imagination, but her fur looked a little shinier today. The rip in her ear looked to be healing.

Jo crouched down beside him and scratched Lucy's neck. Even Kevin bent down to pet the dog. Sam glanced back at Tyler's empty desk in the corner, then at his crew now huddled around Lucy. They were happy, laughing. Even the dog was smiling. Maybe things were looking up for the White Rock Police Department.

EPILOGUE

T*wo weeks later...*

SAM PUSHED the stack of resumes onto Jo's desk, nudging the white donut bag aside. "I want you to look through these. I only see three applicants that would be good for the job, but I want to get your take on it."

"Sure thing." Jo leaned back in her chair, slapping her feet up on the open desk drawer. Things had been quiet since they'd closed the Palmer murder case.

They'd had the usual small-town disturbances. Finding the owners of lost pets, arbitrating problems between neighbors, even solving the fascinating case of the missing milk bottles from Mrs. Murphy's steps. It turned out some bored kids had been playing pranks on her.

But, even though it was quiet, things were looming in the future.

"You going to the town council meeting tonight?" Jo asked as if sensing Sam's gloomy thoughts.

That night, the town council was meeting on a rezoning law. Thorne wanted to rezone a parcel of land he'd purchased so he could continue on the build-out of his resort. Sam was alarmed at the rate that Thorne was buying up properties from the old-timers. He suspected there might be some strong-arming or at least hard persuasion going on to get that land but had no way to prove it.

"You bet. I don't know who Dupont thinks he's kidding. He can't keep influencing the council members so that Thorne can ruin the land and build more hotels and restaurants."

"Tell me about it." Jo glanced out the window. "The scenery is so beautiful here. I'd hate to see it turn into a city."

"It's not gonna. Not if I can help it."

"*Woof.*"

"Even Lucy agrees." Sam crouched down and patted the dog. Lucy was now a permanent fixture due to the grant. Dupont had stopped complaining about her when he'd seen how much the locals loved the idea of a police dog in town.

For Dupont, it was all about the votes, but in this case it also worked in Sam's favor. Of course, Dupont had taken the credit for getting the K-9 grant. Reese played along—she was happy just to have saved Lucy.

Sam had taken to bringing Lucy home with him. He'd gotten accustomed to having the dog as company. She was better company than either of his ex-wives, just as Mick had predicted. She never talked back, was always happy to see him, and didn't expect him to take her out to dinner.

Jo opened the manila folder and started shuffling through the resumes. "I don't know. It seems disloyal somehow to be hiring someone else in Tyler's place."

They both glanced over at the empty desk. Lucy must have agreed with them. She trotted over and started sniffing around then looked back at Sam and whined.

"I know. Even Lucy senses the loss. But we have to fill the opening," Sam said. "Maybe we can get a different desk for the new person."

"*Woof.*" Lucy scratched at the corner of the desk.

"Are you hungry?" Sam glanced at her dish. He'd fed her just a few hours ago.

Lucy kept scratching and looking back at Sam with those whiskey-brown eyes as if she was trying to tell him something.

"Looks like she's after something," Jo said. "Did you ever clean out Tyler's desk?"

Sam nodded solemnly. Kevin had done that job shortly after Tyler died. He'd handed all of Tyler's notebooks and all his notes for the various cases to Sam. The desk was empty.

"Well, I don't know what she's after," Jo said. "Maybe some old food stuck in the bottom of a drawer?"

"*Woof!*" Lucy's scratching became more persistent. She shoved her nose into the three-inch space under the bank of drawers on the side of the desk and sniffed loudly.

Sam went over and crouched down beside her. "What are you doing? Is something under there?"

"*Woof!*"

Sam pressed his cheek to the cold marble floor so he could get a better look at the bottom of the drawer. As if to encourage him, Lucy pressed her snout under the desk too, looking sideways out of the corner of her eye at him.

The desk was old, made of solid wood, not like the new particleboard crap. Even the bottom of the drawer was old oak. Except for a small piece of metal that glinted gold. He wedged his hand under, his fingertips brushing the smooth surface of packing tape and thin bump of something the tape was holding. He peeled the tape away, and something small and metal clinked onto the marble floor. He grabbed it.

Jo had come over and was squatting next to him.

"What is it?"

He pulled it out and opened up his hand. A small gold key tarnished and pitted with rust gleamed in his palm. The numbers 317 were engraved on the rounded top.

Jo plucked it out of his hand. "What is this? A post-office key?"

They both looked back at the row of post-office boxes. Those old boxes didn't take keys—they were a combination lock with two dials on the front. And besides, they didn't need a key to get into those boxes. The backs were open.

"Or a safety deposit box, or locker key? Those types of keys are all this size with numbers on them." Sam took the key back and flipped it over in his hand. "It would be impossible to tell where it came from."

"How long do you think it's been under the desk?" Jo looked up at Sam. Their eyes locked. "Do you think Tyler put this here?"

Sam got that tightness in his chest. The feeling that told him this was something important. That this was something he needed to investigate. "Hard to say. These desks are left over from the post office. The key looks old. So anyone could've put it here, but..."

"Yeah, I know. It seems awfully strange. I don't think this is something we should just put off as coincidence."

Sam stood up and glanced back at the empty desk, a

feeling of foreboding darkening his thoughts. "But if it was Tyler who hid this key under the desk, then that begs the question... what the hell had Tyler been up to before he was killed?"

****

MORE BOOKS in the Sam Mason Mystery Series:

Keeping Secrets (book 2)
Exposing Truths (book 3)
Betraying Trust (Book 4)
Killing Dreams (Book 5)

JOIN my readers list to get new release notifications:
https://ladobbsreaders.gr8.com

DID you know that I write mysteries under other names? Join the LDobbs reader group on Facebook and find out! It's a fun group where I give out inside scoops on my books and we talk about reading!
https://www.facebook.com/groups/ldobbsreaders

ALSO BY L. A. DOBBS

Sam Mason Mysteries

***

Telling Lies (Book 1)

Keeping Secrets (Book 2)

Exposing Truths (Book 3)

Betraying Trust (Book 4)

Killing Dreams (Book 5)

Rockford Security Systems (Romantic Suspense)

*Formerly published with same titles under my pen name Lee Anne Jones

Deadly Betrayal (Book 1)

Fatal Games (Book 2)

Treacherous Seduction (Book 3)

Calculating Desires (Book 4)

Wicked Deception (Book 5)

Criminal Intentions (Book 6)

ABOUT THE AUTHOR

L. A. Dobbs also writes light mysteries as USA Today Bestselling author Leighann Dobbs. Lee has had a passion for reading since she was old enough to hold a book, but she didn't put pen to paper until much later in life. After a twenty-year career as a software engineer, she realized you can't make a living reading books, so she tried her hand at writing them and discovered she had a passion for that, too! She lives in New Hampshire with her husband, Bruce, their trusty Chihuahua mix, Mojo, and beautiful rescue cat, Kitty.

Her book "Dead Wrong" won the "Best Mystery Romance" award at the 2014 Indie Romance Convention.

Her book "Ghostly Paws" was the 2015 Chanticleer Mystery & Mayhem First Place category winner in the Animal Mystery category.

Join her VIP Readers group on Facebook:
https://www.facebook.com/groups/ldobbsreaders

Find out about her L. A. Dobbs Mysteries at:

http://www.ladobbs.com

This is a work of fiction.

None of it is real. All names, places, and events are products of the
author's imagination. Any resemblance to real names, places, or
events are purely coincidental, and should not be construed as being
real.